Apophis's guides

Apophis's guides

Matthew Petchinsky

A pophis's guides:
Witch's Spellbook Crafting Guide for Halloween
By: Matthew Petchinsky

Introduction

Welcome to the **Witch's Spellbook Crafting Guide for Halloween**—your journey into the mystical art of creating a spellbook that resonates with the magic of the season. Whether you are a seasoned witch or a curious beginner, this guide is designed to help you craft a personal spellbook, also known as a "grimoire" or "Book of Shadows," filled with your unique magic. Within these pages, you will discover everything from selecting the perfect book base and designing its cover to filling it with spells, rituals, and symbols that embody your magical practice. By the end of this guide, you will hold in your hands a beautiful spellbook, charged with intention and ready to assist in your spiritual journey.

Overview of the Guide: Purpose and Theme

This guide will walk you through the entire process of crafting a spellbook, offering creative inspiration and practical tips for each step. With Halloween approaching—a time when the veil between worlds is said to be at its thinnest—there is no better time to begin crafting your spellbook. The Halloween season brings an enchanting atmosphere, making it the ideal backdrop for imbuing your book with magical energy. The purpose of this guide is to inspire you to create a spellbook that is not only a repository of knowledge but also a reflection of your personal journey into witchcraft and magic. As you work through each chapter, you will learn how to transform a simple notebook into a sacred text, exploring various aspects of spellcrafting along the way.

The Magic of Spellbook Crafting: Why Create Your Own Spellbook?

The act of creating a spellbook is a powerful ritual in itself. Crafting your own spellbook allows you to infuse your magic into every page, making it a living document that evolves with you. While there are countless pre-made books of spells available, nothing quite compares to the energy and connection that comes from creating your own.

A spellbook serves as a personal archive of your magical knowledge, experiences, and spells. It becomes a sacred space where you can document your rituals, record your dreams, and write down the spells that work best for you. It is a reflection of your magical practice, whether you are drawn to herbal magic, astrology, moon phases, or elemental spells. Moreover, a handmade spellbook can act as a protective talisman, holding the energy you have put into it, and shielding you as you journey through the mystical realms. Crafting your own spellbook empowers you to take control of your magic, make it your own, and establish a deeper connection with the world around you.

Tools, Materials, and Basics for Spellbook Crafting

Before diving into the crafting process, it's essential to gather the right tools and materials. The supplies you choose can greatly influence the spellbook's aesthetic and magical energy, so take the time to select items that resonate with you. Here's a basic list to get you started:

- **Base Book:** The foundation of your spellbook can be anything from a blank journal, sketchbook, or leather-bound notebook to a handmade journal with parchment paper. Choose a book that feels special to you and fits the theme you envision for your spellbook.
- **Writing Tools:** Opt for pens, markers, and inks that reflect your intention. Many witches prefer to use special inks, such as those made with herbs or natural pigments. Consider using fountain pens, quills, or even metallic markers for a magical touch.
- **Decorative Elements:** Gather materials like paints, stickers, washi tape, pressed flowers, stamps, and sigils for embellishing the pages. Ribbons, charms, and crystals can also be added to the cover for extra magic.
- **Glue and Adhesives:** Use high-quality adhesives for attaching elements like dried herbs, sigils, or charms to the pages. Consider using double-sided tape for a clean, easy application.
- **Scissors and Cutting Tools:** For cutting paper, ribbons, and other decorative elements. A precision knife can be useful for intricate designs.

This is just a starting point. Feel free to customize your tools and materials to match your personal style and the magical themes you wish to explore in your spellbook. As you gather your supplies, remember that the intention behind each choice matters. Selecting tools and materials that resonate with you will imbue your spellbook with a personal energy that strengthens its magic.

A Brief History of Witchcraft and Spellbooks

The tradition of using spellbooks is ancient, with roots that stretch back to the earliest forms of magic and witchcraft. In many cultures, wise folk and healers would record their knowledge of herbs, charms, and rituals in manuscripts that were passed down through generations. In medieval Europe, spellbooks—often called grimoires—were considered to be repositories of secret knowledge, containing instructions for casting spells, summoning spirits, and divining the future.

Over time, spellbooks evolved to reflect the individual practices of their creators. While some focused on alchemy and astrology, others recorded incantations, herbal remedies, and talismans for protection. During the Renaissance, grimoires became more widely known and were often written in elaborate scripts with detailed illustrations. With the rise of modern witchcraft movements in the 20th century, such as Wicca, the tradition of keeping a "Book of Shadows" became an essential part of many practitioners' lives. These spellbooks were no longer mere collections of spells; they were personalized records of spiritual experiences, rituals, and magical wisdom.

Today, spellbooks continue to be cherished by witches and magical practitioners worldwide. They serve as a bridge between the past and the present, linking modern witches to the rich history of magic. By creating your own spellbook, you are participating in this long-standing tradition, contributing to the evolving tapestry of witchcraft.

Crafting Safety: How to Handle Materials Safely and Respectfully

As you embark on your spellbook crafting journey, it's important to practice safety and respect for the materials you work with. Many crafting supplies, such as paints, inks, and adhesives, can be messy or potentially harmful if not handled properly. Here are some guidelines to ensure a safe crafting experience:

- **Protect Your Work Area:** Lay down newspaper or a plastic sheet to protect your workspace from spills and stains. Use gloves when working with potentially hazardous materials like ink or glue.
- **Use Non-toxic Supplies:** Whenever possible, choose non-toxic, eco-friendly materials for crafting. Natural inks, herbal dyes, and plant-based glues are safer options and align with many witches' respect for the earth.
- **Be Cautious with Sharp Tools:** Always handle scissors, knives, and other cutting tools with care. Keep them out of reach of children and store them safely when not in use.
- **Respect the Magical Elements:** If you include herbs, crystals, or other natural elements in your spellbook, treat them with respect. Cleanse crystals before use, harvest herbs sustainably, and express gratitude for the gifts of the earth.

By observing these safety practices, you create a respectful and mindful crafting environment. Remember, the process of creating your spellbook is as much about intention as it is about the final product. Approach each step with care, patience, and an open heart, allowing your spellbook to become a true extension of your magical self.

Chapter 1: Choosing the Right Spellbook Base

The base of your spellbook is not just a blank canvas for your magical practice—it is the foundation upon which your intentions, spells, and rituals will be built. Choosing the right spellbook base is an essential step in creating a book that truly reflects your personal path and magical style. In this chapter, we'll explore the various types of spellbook bases, aesthetic choices to enhance the visual theme of your book, and ways to personalize it so that it becomes an extension of your unique magic.

Different Types of Spellbook Bases

Selecting the perfect base for your spellbook depends on your aesthetic preferences, intended use, and the types of materials you plan to work with. Whether you want a simple, easy-to-use notebook or a more sophisticated, ancient-looking grimoire, the following options will help you find a base that resonates with your craft.

1. Blank Notebooks, Journals, and Scrapbooks
Blank Notebooks:

- **Description:** Blank notebooks are one of the most straightforward and versatile options for a spellbook. They come in various sizes, colors, and bindings (spiral-bound, hardback, or softcover) with paper options such as lined, unlined, or dotted. Many witches start their spellbook journey with a simple blank notebook because of its accessibility and ease of use.
- **Advantages:**
  - **Affordability:** Often inexpensive, making them ideal for beginners or those who prefer to create multiple spellbooks over time.
  - **Customizability:** A blank notebook can be easily customized with drawings, stickers, stamps, or even dried flowers and herbs.
  - **Variety:** Available in various colors, patterns, and styles to fit any magical aesthetic.

- **How to Use:** Use sections of the notebook to record different aspects of your practice, such as spells, moon phases, and correspondences. Divide it using tabs, sticky notes, or colored inks. You can enhance the book's magical energy by writing in your own hand, incorporating personal symbols, and using pens or inks that correspond to your intentions (e.g., green ink for prosperity spells).

Journals:

- **Description:** Journals typically offer a more refined and structured option compared to standard blank notebooks. They often feature high-quality paper, sturdy covers, and may include built-in bookmarks or pockets for storing small items. Journals can come in leather-bound, cloth-covered, or printed designs that align with various magical themes.
- **Advantages:**
  - **Durability:** With hardcover options and thick paper, journals are designed to withstand repeated use and handling.
  - **Sophisticated Appearance:** Journals often come with elegant designs, making them feel like a special, magical item.
  - **Organizational Features:** Some journals include pre-drawn sections, blank indexes, or lined pages, which can help structure your spellbook for easy reference.
- **How to Use:** Journals work well for documenting rituals, dreams, and ongoing studies. They provide a neat structure for spells and correspondences, while the thicker paper allows you to incorporate various writing instruments, such as pens, markers, and even watercolor. Add pockets to the inside covers to hold herbs, crystals, or handwritten spells.

Scrapbooks:

- **Description:** Scrapbooks offer ample space for creativity, allowing you to incorporate physical items such as pressed flowers, photographs, and charms. With their larger pages and thicker paper, scrapbooks are perfect for crafting a visual and interactive spellbook that goes beyond mere text.
- **Advantages:**
  - **Creative Freedom:** Scrapbooks provide a larger canvas for you to create full-page magical spreads, incorporating drawings, collages, and mixed media elements.
  - **Mixed Media Use:** Their thick pages can support various crafting materials, including paints, inks, and glued-in items like ribbons or charms.
  - **Personal Touch:** Ideal for witches who prefer a hands-on, artistic approach to spellbook creation.
- **How to Use:** Create elaborate page spreads dedicated to specific spells or magical correspondences. Decorate each page with borders, stamps, and watercolor illustrations. Include envelopes or pockets within the scrapbook to store sigils, written intentions, and other magical items. Use different types of paper—such as parchment, vellum, or cardstock—to add visual and textural variety.

2. Leather-bound Books, Handmade Paper, and Aged Paper for an Authentic Look
Leather-bound Books:

- **Description:** Leather-bound books embody the traditional image of an ancient grimoire, giving your spellbook an aura of timelessness and mystery. These books often feature durable leather covers, sometimes embossed with intricate designs, along with high-quality, thick pages suitable for writing, sketching, and adding decorations.
- **Advantages:**
    ○ **Durability:** Leather-bound covers protect the contents, ensuring that your spellbook will last through years of use.
    ○ **Aesthetic Appeal:** They exude an old-world charm, making your spellbook feel like a magical heirloom or an ancient tome filled with secrets.
    ○ **Enhancements:** Some leather-bound books come with ribbon bookmarks, clasps, or wrap-around straps to secure your writings.
- **How to Use:** Leather-bound books are ideal for witches who wish to create a comprehensive grimoire that documents their entire magical journey. Decorate the cover with sigils, gemstones, or charms that reflect the book's purpose. Inside, use fine-tipped pens, inks, or calligraphy to record spells, rituals, and magical correspondences. Consider inscribing protective symbols or blessings on the front and back covers to enchant the book.

Handmade Paper Books:

- **Description:** Handmade paper books offer a rustic, natural feel that enhances the connection to earth-based practices. Each page is uniquely textured and varies slightly in color, adding character and authenticity to your spellbook. Handmade paper is often thicker, making it suitable for painting, drawing, and writing with a variety of inks.
- **Advantages:**
  - **Artisanal Quality:** Handmade paper creates a sense of craftsmanship, reflecting the personal effort you put into your magical work.
  - **Natural and Eco-Friendly:** Many handmade papers are made using recycled materials, herbs, or natural fibers, aligning with earth-centered magical practices.
  - **Enhanced Sensory Experience:** The texture of hand-made paper adds a tactile element to your spellcrafting, making each entry feel more intentional.
- **How to Use:** Handmade paper books work well for visual elements, such as botanical illustrations, spell diagrams, and sigils. Use paints, colored inks, and pressed herbs to enhance the natural beauty of the pages. Personalize the book further by staining the edges with herbal tea or infusing the pages with essential oils.

Aged Paper for an Authentic Look:

- **Description:** Aged paper gives your spellbook the appearance of an ancient, time-worn grimoire. You can either purchase books with pre-aged pages or age them yourself using techniques like tea staining, burning edges, or crumpling.
- **Advantages:**
  - **Mystical Aura:** Aged paper creates the impression that your spellbook contains centuries-old wisdom, heightening its mystical energy.
  - **Customizable Aging:** You have full control over how aged the paper looks, allowing you to craft the exact aesthetic you desire.
- **How to Use:** Write spells and rituals in ink for an authentic feel. To personalize, include calligraphy, sketches, and pressed herbs. For added enchantment, consider adding wax seals to select pages or burning sigils into the paper's edges.

Aesthetic Choices: Selecting a Color Scheme and Theme

Choosing a color scheme and theme for your spellbook enhances its visual appeal and helps imbue the book with the specific energy of your practice. Here are some popular themes and how to incorporate them:

- **Gothic:** If you are drawn to dark, mysterious aesthetics, choose a color palette of black, deep purples, and blood reds. Use leather-bound or aged-paper books, and add silver or black embellishments such as lace, feathers, or metal charms. Decorate pages with hand-drawn symbols, gothic fonts, and borders of thorns or ivy.
- **Cottagecore:** For a nature-inspired, earthy theme, opt for soft pastels, greens, and earthy browns. Choose a book with a cloth cover, or a journal with natural, unbleached paper. Adorn the pages with pressed flowers, leaf imprints, and watercolor illustrations of herbs, animals, and countryside scenery.
- **Elemental:** Align your spellbook with the four elements (Earth, Air, Fire, Water) by selecting colors and materials that correspond to each. For Earth, use greens and browns with a leather-bound base. For Air, choose light blues, whites, and delicate papers. Fire can incorporate reds, oranges, and golds, with burnt edges or flame-inspired designs. Water-themed spellbooks might feature blues, silvers, and iridescent inks.

Personalizing Your Book: Adding Symbols, Sigils, and Embell-ishments to Make it Unique

Once you've chosen your base and theme, it's time to personalize your spellbook. Infusing your energy into its design not only makes the book uniquely yours but also strengthens its magical potency.

- **Adding Symbols and Sigils:** Draw or paint symbols of pro-tection, power, or personal significance on the cover and pages. Create your own sigils by combining meaningful symbols, or use traditional symbols like pentagrams, elemental signs, or astrologi-cal glyphs. Place these symbols on the first page to act as a magical safeguard for your book.
- **Embellishments:** Attach charms, crystals, or ribbons to the cover for added magic. Use adhesive gems, metallic stickers, or glitter to create a starry sky effect. Inside the book, you can glue small envelopes or pouches to store magical items, such as feath-ers, petals, or fragments of parchment with written intentions.
- **Customized Bookmarks:** Add ribbon or cord bookmarks to mark frequently used sections or ongoing spellwork. Choose col-ors corresponding to different types of magic (e.g., green for pros-perity, red for love) and attach small charms or beads to the ends for a magical touch.
- **Title Page and Dedication:** Create a title page with the spell-book's name, such as "Book of Shadows," "Grimoire of [Your Name]," or something more unique like "Whispers of the Moon." Include a dedication, blessing, or invocation to set the tone and purpose of the spellbook. This page can become a ritual in itself, sealing the book's magical energy.

Your spellbook is a deeply personal creation. The base you choose, the theme you select, and the symbols you add all contribute to its power. Take your time crafting a spellbook that not only aligns with your magical path but also inspires you every time you open its pages.

Chapter 2: Creating the Spellbook Cover

The cover of your spellbook is not only the first thing you see, but it also sets the tone for the magic contained within. A carefully crafted cover serves as a protective shield for your book and symbolizes the intentions and energies you wish to infuse into your practice. Whether you prefer a minimalist design or an ornate masterpiece, creating your spellbook cover is a chance to express your personal magic. In this chapter, we will explore various ways to design the cover, materials you can use, and tips for adding magical elements to transform your book into a sacred vessel.

Designing the Cover: Ideas for Engraving, Etching, or Painting

Creating an enchanting cover begins with selecting a design that resonates with your magical intentions. Here are some ideas and techniques to inspire your creativity:

1. Engraving and Etching:

- **Wooden or Leather Covers:** If you've chosen a spellbook with a wooden or leather cover, engraving or etching is a fantastic way to create an intricate and timeless design. You can use wood-burning tools to etch symbols, sigils, or runes into the cover. For leather-bound books, use a leather engraving tool or a pyrography pen to imprint patterns, symbols, or your spellbook's title.
  - ◦ **Design Ideas:** Etch a pentacle, crescent moon, or elemental symbols to signify the book's magical focus. Consider incorporating personal sigils or sacred geometric patterns that hold specific meaning for your practice.
  - ◦ **Tips:** Before engraving or etching, sketch your design lightly with a pencil. Practice on a scrap piece of wood or leather to get a feel for the tool. When working on leather, ensure the surface is clean and moisten it slightly to make engraving easier.

2. Painting:

- **Acrylic Paints for Hardcovers:** Use acrylic paints to bring color and life to your spellbook cover. Acrylics work well on most surfaces, including cardboard, wood, leather, and vinyl. For a magical touch, consider using metallic paints (gold, silver, or copper) to add shimmer and mystique to your design.
  - ◦ **Design Ideas:** Paint celestial themes like stars, moons, and galaxies, or nature-inspired designs such as vines, flowers, and forest scenes. Create a sigil or magical symbol at the center, surrounded by ornamental designs or mandalas to represent the book's energy.
  - ◦ **Techniques:** Layer different colors to create depth and texture. For an aged look, use a "dry brush" technique by lightly brushing a darker or metallic color over the edges of the cover. Add dots, lines, and swirls with fine brushes to create intricate details.
  - ◦ **Sealing the Design:** Once the paint dries, seal the cover with a matte or glossy finish to protect your artwork. Spray-on acrylic sealers are ideal for this purpose, ensuring that your design remains vibrant and intact.

3. Adding Texture:

- **Embossing:** Use embossing techniques to raise symbols or designs on the cover, giving it a three-dimensional look. Apply embossing powder over a stamped or hand-drawn design, then use a heat tool to melt the powder, creating a raised, glossy pattern.
    - ◦ **Embossing Ideas:** Emboss alchemical symbols, zodiac signs, or the phases of the moon. You can also emboss the title of your spellbook, making it a prominent feature on the cover.
- **Stencils and Decoupage:** Use stencils to paint patterns, sigils, or symbols onto the cover, ensuring a clean and precise design. Alternatively, decoupage printed images or symbols onto the cover using Mod Podge or a similar adhesive. This method allows for layering different elements, such as floral patterns, mystical animals, or images of tarot cards.

Materials for the Cover: Cloth, Leather, Vinyl, and Other Textures

The material of your spellbook cover greatly influences its overall appearance, durability, and feel. Here are some popular materials and tips for working with each:

1. Cloth Covers:

- **Description:** Cloth covers add a soft, comforting texture to your spellbook. They can range from velvet, linen, and cotton to more luxurious fabrics like brocade or silk. Cloth covers are ideal for those who want a book that feels gentle to the touch and resonates with a cottagecore, nature-based aesthetic.
- **How to Apply:** To cover your spellbook with cloth, cut a piece of fabric slightly larger than the book's dimensions. Apply fabric glue to the cover, then carefully smooth the fabric over the surface, pressing out any wrinkles or air bubbles. Tuck the edges inside the covers and secure them with glue or double-sided tape. For an added touch, attach lace trim, embroidery, or fabric patches to create a layered effect.
- **Decorative Ideas:** Embroider symbols or sigils onto the fabric cover for a personal touch. Attach pressed flowers, leaves, or beads to the cloth for a nature-inspired, enchanted appearance.

2. Leather Covers:

- **Description:** Leather-bound covers are classic and durable, giving your spellbook an aura of timelessness. Leather can be left plain for a minimalist, natural look, or decorated with engravings, paint, and attachments for a more elaborate design.
- **How to Work with Leather:** For an existing leather-bound book, use a leather engraver or pyrography pen to etch symbols and patterns. For additional customization, you can paint designs

using leather paint, which adheres to the surface without crack-
ing.
- **Decorative Ideas:** Attach metal charms, crystals, or small brass
accents to the leather for a mystical, ancient feel. Consider wrapping the book with a leather cord and adding a metal clasp or lock
for an extra layer of protection and mystery.

3. Vinyl and Synthetic Covers:

- **Description:** Vinyl and other synthetic materials are durable and
water-resistant, making them suitable for those who carry their
spellbooks frequently. These covers are often smooth and sleek,
allowing for easy customization with paint, decals, and stickers.
- **How to Personalize:** Vinyl covers work well with acrylic paints,
markers, and metallic pens. You can also use adhesive decals, stickers, or washi tape to decorate the cover without permanently al-
tering it.
- **Decorative Ideas:** Apply holographic vinyl stickers, moon
phases, or constellations for a cosmic theme. Create a border
around the edges using metallic washi tape to frame the design.

Incorporating Magical Elements: Charms, Crystals, and Herbs for Decoration and Protection

Adding magical elements to your spellbook cover not only enhances its appearance but also infuses it with protective and energetic properties. Here are some ideas for incorporating charms, crystals, and herbs into your cover design:

1. Charms:

- **Types of Charms:** Choose symbols that resonate with your magical intentions, such as pentagrams for protection, moons for intuition, or keys for unlocking secrets. You can also select charms representing deities, animals, or elements significant to your practice.
- **Attachment Methods:** Sew or glue charms directly onto fabric covers. For leather-bound or vinyl covers, use a small hole punch to create openings for threading charms with leather cords or ribbons. If your spellbook has a wrap-around closure, attach charms to the ends of the cord for added decoration.
- **Magical Purpose:** Before attaching charms, cleanse and charge them with your intentions. Visualize the charm's energy blending with the book's cover, creating a protective shield around its contents.

2. Crystals:

- **Crystal Selection:** Choose crystals based on their magical properties. Amethyst enhances intuition, clear quartz amplifies intentions, and black tourmaline offers protection. Small, flat stones work best for covers, as they can be securely attached without adding too much bulk.
- **Attachment Methods:** For cloth covers, sew a small pouch onto the front to hold a crystal. For other materials, glue crystals onto the cover using strong adhesive, such as E6000 or epoxy resin. Place crystals around the book's central symbol or arrange them in a pattern, like a pentacle or crescent moon.
- **Magical Purpose:** Before attaching, cleanse the crystals and charge them with your desired energy. Visualize the crystals emanating protective energy that envelops the spellbook.

3. Herbs:

- **Herb Selection:** Incorporate dried herbs known for their protective and magical properties, such as sage, rosemary, lavender, or bay leaves. These can be attached to the cover in bundles, sachets, or as part of a decorative wreath.
- **Attachment Methods:** For cloth covers, sew a small sachet of dried herbs and attach it with a ribbon or glue. You can also weave herbs into a small wreath or braid and secure it onto the cover using glue or thread.
- **Magical Purpose:** Bless the herbs with your intentions before attaching them, asking for their protection and guidance. Incorporating herbs into the cover adds a sensory element, providing both visual beauty and a gentle aroma.

DIY Cover Tips: Using Wax Seals, Ribbons, and Pendants
Enhance your spellbook cover with simple yet powerful elements that add both aesthetic beauty and magical protection.
1. Wax Seals:

- **How to Use:** Create wax seals using a sealing wax stick and a stamp. Drip melted wax onto the cover (or a removable paper embellishment), then press the stamp into the wax to form a seal. Choose stamps with magical symbols like pentacles, crescent moons, or personalized sigils.
- **Decorative Ideas:** Use different colored waxes to correspond with specific energies (e.g., green for abundance, purple for spirituality). Consider adding a wax seal over a protective sigil on the first page to symbolize that the book is guarded and private.

2. Ribbons:

- **How to Use:** Attach ribbons to the spine of your spellbook to act as bookmarks or decorative elements. Select ribbons in colors that align with your magical intentions—black for protection, red for courage, or blue for tranquility.
- **Decorative Ideas:** Tie ribbons around the book's cover and knot small charms or beads onto the ends. Weave multiple ribbons together to create a colorful braid that wraps around the book as a closure.

3. Pendants:

- **How to Use:** Attach pendants to the cover or spine of the book. Use symbols such as keys, moons, or ancient runes to invoke their magical energies. Pendants can be sewn, glued, or threaded onto cords that wrap around the book.
- **Magical Purpose:** Pendants serve as protective amulets for your spellbook, acting as a physical representation of your intentions and energies. Enchant the pendant before attaching it, visualizing it as a guardian of your magical knowledge.

By taking the time to design and craft a spellbook cover that resonates with your magical practice, you create a powerful, personalized tool. The cover is more than just decoration—it serves as a protective boundary and a manifestation of your intentions. As you work on your spellbook cover, infuse it with care, love, and focused intention, allowing it to become a sacred vessel for your magical journey.

Chapter 3: Organizing the Spellbook

A well-organized spellbook serves as an invaluable tool for any magical practitioner, allowing you to quickly access spells, correspondences, rituals, and notes. The structure you give your spellbook can influence your magical practice, making it easier to record and revisit your experiences. In this chapter, we will explore different sections to include, how to create a table of contents, use tabs or dividers, and incorporate journal entries. The goal is to design a spellbook that not only serves as a magical repository but also evolves with your journey.

Sections to Include: Spells, Potions, Rituals, Moon Phases, Herbs, and Crystals

Your spellbook should reflect your personal magical practices and interests. While you can include a wide range of topics, it's essential to structure these elements into distinct sections to keep your book organized. Below are some common sections you may want to consider incorporating:

1. Spells

- **Purpose:** This section is the heart of most spellbooks. Here, you'll record all your spells, including those you've created, adapted, or learned from other sources.
- **How to Organize:** Organize your spells by intention (e.g., protection, love, prosperity) or by element (e.g., earth-based spells, water spells). Each spell entry should include the name of the spell, its purpose, ingredients, step-by-step instructions, and any associated incantations. You can also add a notes section to record the date you performed the spell and its outcome.
- **Additional Tips:** Leave space for new spells you might develop over time. Consider using symbols or small drawings to accompany each spell, helping to evoke its energy.

2. Potions and Brews

- **Purpose:** If potion-making is part of your practice, dedicate a section to recording your recipes. This can include herbal teas, tinctures, oils, and magical bath salts.
- **How to Organize:** Categorize potions by their purpose, such as healing, protection, love, or purification. For each potion, list the ingredients, quantities, and preparation method. Include information about the potion's intended use, shelf life, and any associated rituals.
- **Additional Tips:** If using herbs or essential oils, note their correspondences in this section. Add warnings or special instructions, such as "do not ingest" for certain potions.

3. Rituals and Ceremonies

- **Purpose:** Rituals mark significant events in the magical calendar, including Sabbats, Esbats, and other personal ceremonies. Use this section to document detailed instructions for rituals you perform regularly or those you've created for specific occasions.
- **How to Organize:** Consider organizing by the type of ritual (e.g., moon rituals, seasonal celebrations) or by the calendar date (e.g., Samhain, Beltane). Include the purpose of the ritual, materials needed, steps, chants, and any specific correspondences (e.g., crystals, herbs).
- **Additional Tips:** Include personal reflections after performing each ritual to document your experiences and any insights gained.

4. Moon Phases

- **Purpose:** The moon's phases have a profound impact on magical workings. This section provides a reference for how different phases can be used to amplify spellwork.
- **How to Organize:** Create a moon phase calendar or chart, detailing the qualities of each phase—new moon, waxing crescent, full moon, waning gibbous, etc. Include information on which types of spells are most effective during each phase (e.g., new moon for new beginnings, full moon for manifestation).
- **Additional Tips:** Leave space for noting lunar eclipses, blood moons, and other celestial events. You might also include moon-based rituals, such as charging crystals or moon water preparation.

5. Herbs and Crystals

- **Herbs Section:**
  - **Purpose:** This section acts as a reference guide for herbs and plants used in your spellwork, potions, and rituals. Document their magical properties, correspondences, and uses.
  - **How to Organize:** Alphabetically list each herb, including its scientific name, magical properties (e.g., protection, love), and how you use it in your practice (e.g., teas, incense, sachets). Include a drawing or pressed specimen of each herb for visual reference.
  - **Additional Tips:** Note any safety information, such as whether the herb is toxic or should be used with caution. You can also include harvest dates or notes on sourcing.

-
-
-

- **Crystals Section:**
  - ◦ **Purpose:** Similar to the herbs section, the crystals section serves as a quick guide to the stones and minerals you work with, detailing their properties and uses in magic.
  - ◦ **How to Organize:** List crystals alphabetically or by color. For each crystal, include its properties, correspondences (e.g., chakra associations, elemental ties), and instructions for use (e.g., in rituals, as talismans).
  - ◦ **Additional Tips:** Include information on how to cleanse and charge each crystal. If you perform specific rituals with your crystals, make a note of those practices here.

Creating a Table of Contents: Indexing for Easy Navigation

A table of contents is crucial for a comprehensive spellbook, particularly as it grows over time. A well-structured table of contents allows you to locate specific spells, rituals, or references quickly.

1. How to Create a Table of Contents:

- **Placement:** Create the table of contents on the first few pages of your spellbook. Reserve one or two pages, depending on the number of sections you plan to include.
- **Indexing:** Number each page of your spellbook as you fill it in. As you add content, update the table of contents with the section name, title, and corresponding page number (e.g., "Protection Spells – Page 15").
- **Subsections:** For larger sections, such as "Spells" or "Herbs," list subsections under the main heading. For example:
  - ◦ **Spells:**
    - ▪ Love Spell – Page 10
    - ▪ Prosperity Spell – Page 12
    - ▪ Protection Spell – Page 14

- **Additional Tips:** If your spellbook is a loose-leaf or binder-style format, consider creating a contents page that can be updated and reprinted as needed.

2. Creative Elements:

- **Visual Aids:** Use symbols, doodles, or color coding in the table of contents to make navigation easier. For example, use a green dot next to all herb-related sections or a crescent moon symbol next to moon phase references.
- **Bookmarks:** Add ribbon bookmarks to your spellbook to mark frequently used sections. Choose different colors to correspond with different sections (e.g., red for rituals, blue for moon phases).

Using Tabs or Dividers: Making Sections Accessible

Tabs and dividers are practical tools for sectioning off your spellbook, making it easier to flip directly to the desired page.

1. Tabs:

- **How to Use:** Purchase adhesive tabs from a stationery store, or create your own using cardstock and tape. Write the name of each section (e.g., "Spells," "Herbs," "Moon Phases") on the tabs and stick them to the edges of the pages.
- **Color Coding:** Use different colors for each section to enhance visual organization. For example, assign green tabs for herbs, purple for crystals, and blue for moon phases.
- **Custom Tabs:** For a personal touch, design your own tabs using cardstock. Draw symbols on each tab corresponding to the section it marks (e.g., a pentacle for the spells section, a moon for the moon phases).

2. Dividers:

- **How to Use:** Dividers work well for binder-style or loose-leaf spellbooks. Use pre-made dividers or create your own using decorative paper or cardstock. Add labels or headings to the top or side of each divider for easy identification.
- **Decorating Dividers:** Personalize dividers by decorating them with symbols, stickers, drawings, or pressed flowers. Incorporate magical elements such as sigils or protective symbols to enhance the energy of each section.

Incorporating Journal Entries: Documenting Rituals, Experiences, and Dreams

In addition to spells and correspondences, including journal entries in your spellbook adds a personal touch and helps you track your growth as a practitioner.

1. Ritual and Spell Documentation:

- **Purpose:** Documenting the rituals and spells you perform allows you to reflect on their outcomes, gain insights into your practice, and improve future workings.
- **How to Record:** For each ritual or spell, include the date, the intention, materials used, steps taken, and any incantations or invocations. After the ritual, record your observations, feelings, and results. Note any signs or omens that occurred during or after the ritual.
- **Reflections:** Periodically review these entries to identify patterns or changes in your practice. You may notice certain moon phases or materials that consistently yield better results.

2. Personal Experiences:

- **Purpose:** Documenting magical experiences, meditations, and intuitive insights helps you keep track of your spiritual journey. This section can include daily affirmations, tarot readings, or messages received during meditation.
- **How to Record:** Include the date, the context of the experience (e.g., "meditation on self-love"), and your thoughts and emotions. Describe any symbols, visions, or sensations that arose during the experience.
- **Reflective Questions:** To deepen your self-awareness, consider adding reflective prompts to your entries, such as "What did I learn from this experience?" or "How can I apply this insight to my practice?"

3. Dream Journal:

- **Purpose:** Dreams are a powerful source of insight and guidance in magic. Recording your dreams can help you identify messages from your subconscious, spirit guides, or the universe.
- **How to Record:** Keep a section of your spellbook dedicated to dreams. Write down your dreams as soon as you wake up, noting any symbols, emotions, or themes. If you practice dream magic, include dream spells, lucid dreaming techniques, and any interpretations or meanings.
- **Analysis:** Over time, review your dream entries to identify recurring symbols or patterns. Use these insights to inform your spellwork and rituals, as dreams often reveal hidden desires, fears, or spiritual guidance.

By organizing your spellbook with sections, tabs, and journal entries, you create a functional and evolving magical record. This structured approach allows you to easily access spells, reference moon phases, and reflect on your experiences, making your spellbook an indispensable part of your practice. As you continue to grow in your craft, your spellbook will expand, becoming a personal archive of your magical journey.

Chapter 4: Crafting Spells and Rituals

A spellbook is more than just a collection of spells; it is a repository of your personal magic, your intentions, and the symbols that resonate with your energy. Crafting spells and rituals for your book allows you to harness the power of your creativity and intuition, making your spell-work unique and deeply personal. In this chapter, we will explore how to create your own spells, format them using symbols and runes, add illustrations to enhance their potency, and decorate the pages to infuse them with beauty and magic.

Writing Spells: How to Create Personalized Spells for Your Book

Creating your own spells is one of the most fulfilling aspects of magical practice. When you write a spell, you're shaping your intentions into words, actions, and symbols that channel energy into a desired outcome. Here's a step-by-step guide on how to craft personalized spells for your spellbook:

1. Set Your Intention

- **Purpose:** The foundation of any spell is its intention—what you want to achieve or manifest. Before writing a spell, take some time to clearly define your intention. Is it for protection, love, prosperity, healing, or something else? The more specific you can be, the better.
- **Journaling:** Consider using your spellbook as a journal to explore your intention in depth. Write down what you want, why you want it, and how you envision the outcome. This reflection can provide clarity and focus as you craft your spell.

2. Choose Your Correspondences

- **Tools and Ingredients:** Select tools, herbs, crystals, colors, and other magical components that align with your intention. For example, rose petals might correspond with love spells, while sage and black tourmaline are often used for protection.
- **Timing:** Consider the timing of the spell. Aligning it with moon phases, days of the week, or specific astrological events can enhance its power. For instance, spells for new beginnings are often performed during the new moon, while spells for release and banishment are best suited for the waning moon.
- **Associations:** Incorporate planetary, elemental, and deity correspondences that resonate with your intention. For example, the element of water is associated with emotions and intuition, making it a good addition to spells involving love or healing.

3. Write the Spell Incantation

- **Simple Language:** When crafting the incantation, use clear and direct language that reflects your intention. Rhyming phrases and poetic forms can add rhythm and focus to the spell, but simplicity can be just as effective. Example: "By earth and fire, air and sea, I call this power forth to me."
- **Present Tense:** Write the incantation as if the outcome is already happening. This reinforces the idea that the spell's intention is already in motion. For example, instead of saying, "I will be safe," use, "I am safe and protected."
- **Affirmative Statements:** Avoid negative phrasing (e.g., "I don't want to feel fear"). Instead, use positive affirmations (e.g., "I am filled with courage and peace").

4. Add Instructions and Actions

- **Step-by-Step Guide:** Write out the spell in a step-by-step format. Include instructions on how to prepare the space, what tools to gather, and how to use each item. This section should detail the physical actions, such as lighting a candle, stirring a potion, or drawing a sigil.
- **Focus and Visualization:** Incorporate steps for visualization or meditation within the spell. For example, you might write, "Close your eyes and visualize a protective light surrounding you," to enhance the spell's effectiveness.

5. Closing the Spell

- **Grounding the Energy:** It's essential to ground the energy after the spellwork to release excess energy and seal the spell's intention. Include a closing statement such as "So mote it be" or "This is my will; it is done." You might also add a ritual gesture, such as extinguishing a candle or ringing a bell, to signify the end of the spell.
- **Thanking:** If you called upon deities, spirits, or elemental forces during the spell, remember to express gratitude in your closing statement. Example: "I thank the spirits of earth and sky for their presence. My work is done."

Spell Formatting: Using Symbolism, Runes, and Handwritten Scripts

How you format and write your spells in your spellbook is just as important as the words themselves. The inclusion of symbols, runes, and handwritten scripts adds layers of meaning and energy to your spells.

1. Using Symbolism

- **Magic Symbols:** Symbols like pentacles, moons, suns, elemental triangles, and astrological glyphs can amplify the spell's power. Include symbols that correspond to the spell's intention; for example, draw a heart for love spells or a spiral for transformation.
- **Placement:** Place symbols at the top of the page as a header, next to specific instructions, or as a border around the spell. For example, draw a series of protective symbols around the edges of a spell for safety.
- **Personal Sigils:** Create and include a personal sigil within the spell. A sigil is a symbol derived from a phrase or intention, designed to focus magical energy. Draw the sigil at the beginning or end of the spell to serve as an anchor for the intention.

2. Incorporating Runes

- **Runic Alphabets:** Runes are ancient symbols used in magical practices, each carrying specific meanings and energies. Incorporate runes into your spells by writing key words in a runic alphabet, such as the Elder Futhark.
- **Runic Placement:** Use runes as an embellishment around the spell or integrate them into the incantation itself. For example, include the rune "Algiz" for protection spells or "Fehu" for abundance spells.
- **Drawing Runes:** Draw runes with a specific color ink that matches your intention. For example, use red ink for spells involving love or passion, and green for prosperity.

3. Handwritten Scripts

- **Calligraphy and Cursive:** Writing your spells in cursive or calligraphy adds an elegant and magical touch to your spellbook. The act of handwriting itself is a form of ritual, focusing your intention as you write.
- **Personal Touch:** Include flourishes, decorative lines, and loops in your handwriting to give each spell a unique look. If using runes or magical alphabets, consider practicing them until you feel comfortable incorporating them seamlessly into your script.
- **Special Inks:** Use colored or magical inks (e.g., ink infused with herbs, crystals, or essential oils) to write your spells. For example, use lavender-infused ink for relaxation spells or rose-infused ink for love spells.

Adding Illustrations: Sketching Magical Symbols, Herbs, and Tools

Illustrations add a visual component to your spells, helping to solidify the intention and energize the spellbook. You don't have to be a professional artist to enhance your spellbook with drawings; simple sketches or doodles can be equally powerful.

1. Sketching Symbols

- **Common Symbols:** Draw common magical symbols, such as pentagrams, moons, triquetras, or zodiac signs, to represent specific energies in the spell. For example, a crescent moon could signify intuition, while a star represents guidance.
- **Sigils:** Design your own sigils and include them as illustrations. Create a step-by-step process for constructing sigils, starting with a phrase that embodies the spell's intention, reducing it to its core components, and transforming it into an abstract symbol.

2. Drawing Herbs and Plants

- **Herbal Correspondences:** If your spell involves herbs, sketch small drawings of the plants alongside the spell. For example, include a lavender sprig for spells of peace, or rosemary for protection.
- **Illustrative Borders:** Use plants and herbs to decorate the borders of the page. Draw intertwining vines, leaves, and flowers to frame the spell, adding an earthy and natural touch.

3. Depicting Tools and Ritual Elements

- **Magical Tools:** Illustrate tools used in the spell, such as candles, wands, crystals, or cauldrons. This not only adds visual interest but also serves as a reference for what you need to gather when performing the spell.
- **Ritual Spaces:** If the spell takes place in a particular setting (e.g., at an altar or in a sacred circle), sketch a simple diagram of the ritual space. Include positions for candles, symbols, and other items to help guide you during the spell.

Decorating the Pages: Using Stickers, Stamps, Pressed Flowers, and Watercolors for an Enchanted Look

Once the spell is written and illustrated, adding decorative elements can enhance the spell's energy and make the page more visually appealing.

1. Using Stickers and Stamps

- **Stickers:** Choose stickers that align with the spell's theme, such as stars, moons, flowers, or magical creatures. Place them strategically around the page to add a touch of whimsy or symbolism.
- **Stamps:** Use rubber stamps to add repeated patterns or symbols. For example, use a stamp of a crescent moon for lunar spells or a star stamp for celestial-themed spells. Experiment with ink colors to match the energy of the spell—gold for success, silver for intuition, or black for protection.

2. Incorporating Pressed Flowers and Herbs

- **Selecting Plants:** Use flowers, leaves, and herbs that correspond to the spell's intention. For example, press a rose petal into the page of a love spell or a sage leaf for a cleansing spell.
- **Attachment:** Glue or tape the pressed flowers and herbs onto the page. If you want to keep the herbs more secure, place them inside a small envelope or affix them beneath a piece of clear tape.
- **Tips:** Ensure that the pressed flowers and herbs are fully dried before attaching them to avoid mold or damage to the spellbook.

3. Adding Watercolors

- **Backgrounds:** Use watercolors to create soft, ethereal backgrounds for your spells. Light washes of color can set the mood—blue for tranquility, red for passion, green for abundance. Let the paint dry completely before writing over it.
- **Accents:** Add watercolor accents, such as swirls, stars, or moon phases, to the margins or corners of the page. Light, translucent layers of watercolor can enhance the magical atmosphere without overshadowing the spell text.

By taking the time to craft your spells and rituals with intention, artistic flair, and personal symbolism, you infuse each page with your unique energy. Your spellbook becomes a living document, reflecting your creativity and dedication to your practice. As you continue to fill your spellbook with spells, illustrations, and decorations, it will grow into a powerful, personal artifact that holds the essence of your magical journey.

Chapter 5: Incorporating Magical Correspondences

Incorporating magical correspondences into your spellbook is essential for deepening your understanding of various magical elements and enhancing the effectiveness of your spellwork. Magical correspondences are the associations that different herbs, crystals, moon phases, and astrological events have with specific energies and intentions. By recording these correspondences in your spellbook, you create a valuable reference that you can consult when crafting spells, rituals, and other magical workings. This chapter will guide you in creating detailed sections for herbal correspondences, crystals and gemstones, moon phases, and astrological references.

Herbal Correspondences: Creating a Section for Herbs, Their Uses, and Magical Properties

Herbs are a fundamental component of many magical practices. They can be used in spells, potions, sachets, baths, and rituals, each carrying unique properties and energies. Documenting herbal correspondences in your spellbook provides a convenient reference for crafting spells and enhancing your knowledge of herbal magic.

1. Setting Up the Herbs Section

- **Layout:** Dedicate several pages or an entire section of your spellbook to herbs. Depending on the size of your spellbook, you can choose to list herbs alphabetically, by their elemental associations (e.g., earth, fire, water, air), or by their magical uses (e.g., protection, love, healing).
- **Index:** If your herbs section will be extensive, create an index at the beginning to help you navigate quickly to specific herbs and their properties.

2. Documenting Individual Herbs

- **Herb Name:** Write the common name of the herb at the top of the page. If known, include its botanical (scientific) name in smaller text for reference.
- **Magical Properties:** List the herb's magical properties and associations. For example, rosemary is associated with protection, purification, and mental clarity, while lavender is linked to peace, love, and sleep.
- **Uses in Magic:** Describe how the herb can be used in spells and rituals. Include various forms, such as fresh, dried, or in essential oil form. For example, you might note that rosemary can be burned as incense for protection or added to bathwater for purification.
- **Correspondences:** Document the herb's elemental (e.g., earth, fire) and planetary (e.g., Mercury, Venus) correspondences, as well as its associations with specific deities or zodiac signs if relevant. These correspondences can help you choose the most effective herbs for particular magical intentions.
- **Illustrations and Specimens:** Include a small illustration or drawing of the herb for visual reference. If possible, press a dried sample of the herb and affix it to the page using clear tape or a small envelope.
- **Cautions:** Include any safety information, such as toxicity, potential skin irritation, or ingestion risks. For example, mistletoe is toxic if ingested, and some essential oils like cinnamon can cause skin irritation if not diluted properly.

3. Creating a Quick-Reference Chart

- **Purpose:** In addition to detailed entries, consider creating a quick-reference chart listing common herbs and their primary properties. For example:

Herb	Primary Properties	Element	Planet
Rosemary	Protection, Purification	Fire	Sun
Lavender	Peace, Love, Sleep	Air	Mercury
Sage	Cleansing, Wisdom	Air	Jupiter
Chamomile	Relaxation, Prosperity	Water	Sun
Rose	Love, Healing, Protection	Water	Venus

This chart allows you to quickly find an herb's properties without needing to flip through detailed entries.

Crystals and Gemstones: Documenting Their Energies and Purposes

Crystals and gemstones are widely used in magic for their unique vibrational energies. Incorporating a crystals and gemstones section into your spellbook will give you a go-to reference when selecting stones for spells, rituals, meditation, and energy work.

1. Setting Up the Crystals Section

- **Organization:** You can organize your crystal section alphabetically, by color, by chakras (e.g., root chakra stones, heart chakra stones), or by their primary uses (e.g., protection, love, healing).
- **Index:** For an extensive crystals section, include an index for easy navigation.

2. Documenting Individual Crystals

- **Crystal Name:** Write the crystal's name prominently at the top of the page. Include any alternative names it may have (e.g., "Amethyst" also known as "The Stone of Sobriety").
- **Properties and Uses:** List the crystal's key properties and associations. For example, amethyst is associated with spiritual growth, protection, and calming energy, while citrine is linked to prosperity, creativity, and joy.
- **Magical Uses:** Describe how the crystal can be used in magical practices. For example, you might note that amethyst can be placed under a pillow to promote restful sleep or worn as a talisman for protection against negative energies.

- **Correspondences:** Include elemental (e.g., water, earth) and planetary (e.g., moon, sun) correspondences, as well as chakra associations. For instance, rose quartz corresponds with the heart chakra and is ruled by Venus, aligning it with love and harmony.
- **Illustrations:** Sketch the crystal or gemstone to provide a visual reference. Add color to the drawing to mimic the crystal's natural appearance, which can be particularly helpful if you own multiple crystals and want to identify them correctly.
- **Care and Cleansing:** Note any special care instructions for the crystal, such as "avoid water" for selenite or "sunlight charging" for citrine. Include cleansing methods, such as smudging with sage, placing in moonlight, or using sound vibrations.

3. Creating a Crystal Grid or Chart

- **Quick-Reference Chart:** Create a chart summarizing common crystals and their properties. For example:

Crystal	Primary Properties	Chakra	Element	Planet
Amethyst	Spirituality, Protection	Third Eye, Crown	Water	Jupiter
Rose Quartz	Love, Compassion	Heart	Water	Venus
Citrine	Abundance, Creativity	Solar Plexus	Fire	Sun
Black Tourmaline	Grounding, Protection	Root	Earth	Saturn
Clear Quartz	Amplification, Clarity	All	Air	Sun

A quick-reference chart helps you select crystals efficiently when crafting spells and rituals.

Moon Phases and Their Influences: Including Charts and Diagrams

The moon has a profound influence on magical practices. Each phase of the moon carries its own energy, affecting the potency and nature of spellwork. Including a moon phase section in your spellbook will guide you in timing your rituals and spells for maximum effect.

1. Understanding the Moon Phases

- **New Moon:** Associated with new beginnings, intentions, and setting goals. Ideal for spells related to starting new projects, personal growth, and manifesting desires.
- **Waxing Crescent:** A time for building energy, growth, and attracting what you desire. Perfect for spells involving motivation, abundance, and prosperity.
- **First Quarter:** Represents action, decision-making, and overcoming obstacles. Use this phase for spells that require courage, determination, and progress.
- **Waxing Gibbous:** A period of refinement and preparation. Great for spells that involve finalizing plans, adjustments, and building momentum.
- **Full Moon:** A time of peak power, manifestation, and illumination. Conduct spells for manifestation, protection, and clarity.
- **Waning Gibbous:** A phase for release, gratitude, and re-evaluation. Ideal for banishing negativity, releasing old habits, and expressing gratitude.
- **Last Quarter:** A time for letting go, forgiveness, and shedding the old. Use this phase for banishing, breaking bad habits, and cleansing.
- **Waning Crescent:** Associated with rest, reflection, and spiritual work. Best for meditation, introspection, and preparing for new cycles.

2. Including Moon Charts and Diagrams

- **Moon Phase Calendar:** Create a lunar calendar that tracks the moon phases throughout the month. You can draw small icons representing each phase and label them with their dates. This calendar will help you plan your spells and rituals according to the moon's energy.
- **Moon Cycle Diagram:** Include a diagram of the moon's cycle, showing the progression from new moon to full moon and back. Label each phase with its corresponding magical focus (e.g., "New Moon – Beginnings," "Full Moon – Manifestation").
- **Correspondence Table:** Create a table summarizing the moon phases and their influences:

Moon Phase	Magical Focus	Suggested Spells
New Moon	Beginnings, Intentions	Manifestation, Goal Setting
Waxing Crescent	Growth, Attraction	Abundance, Prosperity
First Quarter	Action, Overcoming Obstacles	Courage, Motivation
Full Moon	Power, Manifestation	Love, Protection, Clarity
Waning Crescent	Rest, Reflection	Meditation, Dream Work

Astrological References: Incorporating Zodiac Signs, Planetary Alignments, and Retrogrades

Astrology plays a vital role in magical practices. The positions and movements of celestial bodies can significantly influence spellwork. Incorporating astrological references into your spellbook helps you align your magic with cosmic energies.

1. Documenting Zodiac Signs

- **Zodiac Profiles:** Create profiles for each zodiac sign, detailing their elemental associations (fire, earth, air, water), ruling planets, key traits, and areas of influence. For example, Aries (fire) is ruled by Mars, associated with courage, passion, and leadership.
- **Magical Uses:** Describe how each zodiac sign's energy can be used in magic. For example, use Virgo's energy for spells involving organization, healing, and discernment, or Leo's energy for spells that boost confidence and attract success.
- **Zodiac Chart:** Include a zodiac chart showing the signs, their symbols, and ruling planets. This chart provides a quick reference for selecting the best zodiac energy to work with for specific intentions.

2. Planetary Alignments

- **Planetary Profiles:** Dedicate a section to the planets, outlining their astrological and magical influences. For example, Venus rules love, beauty, and harmony, while Saturn governs discipline, structure, and karmic lessons.
- **Correspondences:** Document each planet's elemental and zodiac correspondences, along with associated days of the week and colors. For instance, Venus corresponds with the element of wa-

ter, rules over Libra and Taurus, and is associated with Friday and the color pink.

- **Planetary Hours:** Include a chart of planetary hours, which divides each day into segments ruled by different planets. This chart can help you time your spellwork to harness the appropriate planetary energy.

3. Retrogrades and Their Effects

- **Retrograde Calendar:** Create a calendar tracking the retrograde periods of key planets, especially Mercury, Venus, Mars, Jupiter, and Saturn. Mark the start and end dates of each retrograde to plan your magical activities accordingly.
- **Retrograde Influences:** Write about the typical effects of planetary retrogrades. For example, Mercury retrograde is known for communication issues and technological mishaps, making it a time for introspection rather than launching new projects.
- **Retrograde Spells:** Include spells or rituals tailored to retrograde periods. For example, during Mercury retrograde, focus on spells for protection, clarity, and healing past wounds.

By creating comprehensive sections for herbs, crystals, moon phases, and astrological references, you equip your spellbook with the knowledge to enhance your magic. These correspondences are the keys to aligning your spellwork with the natural and cosmic forces around you. As you continue to explore and add to these sections, your spellbook will become an ever-growing resource of magical wisdom.

Chapter 6: Sealing the Spellbook with Protection

Your spellbook is not just a collection of spells, rituals, and magical knowledge—it is a sacred repository of your energy, experiences, and intentions. As such, it is crucial to protect it from unwanted energies, interference, and prying eyes. Sealing your spellbook with layers of protection ensures that its contents remain secure, enhancing its power and maintaining the integrity of your magic. In this chapter, we will explore various methods to safeguard your spellbook, including crafting protection spells, creating wax seals, incorporating wards and sigils, and performing a blessing ritual to consecrate the book.

Protection Spells: Adding Protection Spells to Safeguard the Book

One of the most effective ways to shield your spellbook is to include protective spells within its pages. Protection spells create an energetic barrier around the book, preventing negative energies or intruders from affecting its contents. Here are a few ideas for crafting protection spells tailored to your spellbook:

1. Protection Charm Spell

- **Ingredients:** A small charm (e.g., a pentacle, an eye, or a key), black thread, salt, and a candle (preferably black or white).
- **Instructions:**
    1. Light the candle and place the charm in front of it. Visualize a protective barrier forming around your spellbook.
    2. Sprinkle salt in a circle around the book, representing a protective boundary.
    3. Wrap the charm with black thread while repeating the following incantation:
       "By the power of earth, fire, water, and air,
       This charm protects with utmost care.

No harm shall enter, no eyes shall see,
This book is sealed, so mote it be."

4. Attach the charm to the cover or spine of the spellbook using glue or thread.
5. Allow the candle to burn out naturally, sealing the spell's energy within the charm.

2. Sigil of Protection Spell

- **Ingredients:** Pen, paper, and a black or purple candle.
- **Instructions:**
  1. On a small piece of paper, draw a protective sigil. Create your sigil by using words or phrases like "Protection," "Secrecy," or "Safe from harm," and convert them into a symbolic design.
  2. Light the candle and focus your intention on the sigil. Visualize it glowing with protective energy.
  3. Place the paper inside the front cover of your spellbook, stating the following incantation:
     "This sigil stands as my shield,
     With power, this book is sealed.
     No eyes shall pry, no harm shall breach,
     This spellbook is guarded, safe from reach."
  4. Allow the candle to burn for a few minutes, infusing the spell with energy. Extinguish the candle, fold the sigil paper, and tuck it securely into the book.

3. Circle of Light Protection

- **Ingredients:** A small mirror, a piece of clear quartz, and white cloth.
- **Instructions:**
  1. Place the mirror on your altar or workspace and put the spellbook on top of it. Place the clear quartz beside the book.
  2. Wrap the spellbook in the white cloth while visualizing a circle of white light surrounding it.
  3. Chant the following:
     "Circle of light, shield and protect,
     Guard this book with utmost respect.
     Reflect all harm, repel the ill,
     This spellbook is sacred, protected by will."
  4. Keep the mirror beneath the book and the quartz on top of it for 24 hours to solidify the protection. Then, remove the items and store the quartz in a pouch with the spellbook for continued protection.

Enchanted Seals: How to Create a Wax Seal for Your Spellbook

Wax seals are a powerful way to physically and energetically seal your spellbook. Creating a wax seal is a ritual act that signifies the spellbook is closed to unwanted influences, guarding its content. Here's how to make a wax seal for your spellbook:

1. Materials for Wax Seal Creation

- Sealing wax (available in various colors; use black for protection, red for strength, or gold for empowerment)
- A seal stamp (preferably with a protective symbol, such as a pentagram, key, or your personal sigil)
- Lighter or matches
- Small bowl of salt (optional, for extra protection)

2. How to Create the Wax Seal

1. **Preparation:** Clear your workspace and set up a small altar with the spellbook in the center. Light a candle to create a focused, sacred space. Sprinkle a circle of salt around the spellbook if you wish to add an extra layer of protection during the sealing.
2. **Melting the Wax:** Hold the sealing wax stick over the spellbook's opening (e.g., near the front or back cover) and use the lighter to melt the end of the wax. Allow several drops of wax to form a small pool on the cover or spine of the book.
3. **Press the Seal:** Immediately press the seal stamp into the melted wax. Hold it in place for a few seconds to let the wax set. While pressing, focus on your intention to protect the book, and say aloud:
   "With this seal, I lock this tome,
   Guarded secrets, safe at home.
   None shall pass without my word,
   By this seal, my will is heard."
4. **Removing the Seal Stamp:** Carefully lift the seal stamp from the wax, revealing the symbol embossed in the seal. Let the wax harden completely before handling the book further.
5. **Charging the Seal:** To enhance the wax seal's potency, hold your hand over the seal and visualize it glowing with protective energy. Infuse it with your intention to guard the spellbook against all intrusions.

3. Tips for Wax Sealing

- **Personal Symbols:** Use a seal stamp with a personal sigil or protective symbol to make the seal uniquely yours.
- **Seal Placement:** You can place the wax seal on the front cover, the spine, or the first page of the book. If you want to reseal the

book each time you use it, consider sealing it with a ribbon wrap and wax at the knot.

Incorporating Wards and Sigils: Drawing Symbols for Secrecy and Security

Symbols, sigils, and wards are powerful tools for adding magical protection to your spellbook. These symbols act as energetic barriers, obscuring the book's content from unwanted eyes and interference.

1. Drawing Protective Symbols

- **Pentacles:** A pentacle is one of the most well-known protective symbols, representing balance and the unity of the elements. Draw a small pentacle on the inside cover or the first page of your spellbook to act as a guardian seal.
- **The Evil Eye:** Draw an eye symbol, sometimes known as the "Evil Eye," to repel negativity and prevent anyone from casting harmful intentions toward your spellbook. Include this symbol on the cover or at the bottom of each page for ongoing protection.
- **Triple Moon:** The triple moon symbol (waxing, full, and waning moons) is a powerful protective charm that honors the phases of the moon and the goddess. It is often used to imbue magical works with the moon's cyclical protection.

2. Crafting and Charging Personal Sigils

- **Create Your Sigil:** To craft a personal sigil for your spellbook, start with a phrase such as "This book is protected" or "Hidden from prying eyes." Remove the vowels and repeating consonants, leaving a set of unique letters. Combine these letters into an abstract, unique symbol.
- **Charging the Sigil:** Place the sigil on your altar and surround it with protective elements (e.g., crystals, salt). Visualize energy

flowing into the sigil, filling it with the power of protection. When you feel the sigil is charged, draw or paint it onto the spellbook's cover, spine, or first page.

- **Sigil Placement:** Draw sigils in hidden places within the spellbook, such as the corners of pages, under the cover flap, or at the back of the book. This adds an extra layer of security by concealing the protective symbols from plain sight.

3. Setting Up Wards

- **Warding Ritual:** Create a ritual for setting up wards around your spellbook. Hold the book in your hands and visualize a barrier of light surrounding it. Chant:
"Wards I set, strong and clear,
Guard this book, none shall peer.
By earth, fire, wind, and sea,
Wards of magic, protect for me."
- **Renewing Wards:** Regularly renew the wards around your spellbook by tracing the symbols with your finger or by sprinkling a circle of salt around the book while chanting the warding spell.

Blessing the Book: Rituals for Consecrating the Spellbook

A blessing ritual consecrates the spellbook, infusing it with positive energy and your personal intent. This process marks the spellbook as a sacred object, enhancing its magical potency and further protecting it from negativity.

1. Preparing for the Blessing Ritual

- **Ingredients:** A white candle, salt, a small bowl of water, and an incense stick (sage, sandalwood, or lavender work well).

- **Sacred Space:** Set up your altar or workspace for the ritual. Place the spellbook in the center, surrounded by the candle, salt, water, and incense.

2. Performing the Blessing Ritual

1. **Cleansing:** Light the incense and pass the spellbook through the smoke, saying:
   "By air and smoke, I cleanse this tome,
   Clearing all, this book's my own."

2. **Elemental Blessing:** Sprinkle a pinch of salt over the book, representing the element of earth, and say:
   "Earth, bless this book with strength and might."
   Dip your fingers into the water and sprinkle a few drops over the book, saying:
   "Water, bless this book with wisdom bright."
   Pass the book over the candle's flame (carefully) and say:
   "Fire, bless this book with power and light."
   Blow gently across the book, invoking air:
   "Air, bless this book with insight and sight."

3. **Empowering:** Place your hands over the book and visualize it surrounded by a protective aura. Chant:
   "Blessed be this book I hold,
   Guarded now as magic unfolds.
   Sealed in light, protected and clear,
   Only love and truth shall near."

4. **Sealing:** Close the book and hold it to your heart. Envision it glowing with protective energy, now consecrated and sealed with your intention.

5. **Completing the Ritual:** Allow the candle to burn for a few minutes before extinguishing it. Store the spellbook in a safe, special place when not in use.

By sealing your spellbook with layers of protection, you create a secure space for your magical knowledge to thrive. The combination of protection spells, enchanted seals, wards, sigils, and blessing rituals fortifies the book, ensuring it remains a powerful, personal, and sacred tool throughout your magical journey.

Chapter 7: Enhancing Your Spellbook with Mystical Elements

A spellbook is a living, evolving tool that not only contains magical information but also serves as an expression of your creativity and personal practice. Enhancing your spellbook with mystical elements can amplify its power, turning it into an even more potent and personal artifact. This chapter explores how to create enchanted inks, incorporate interactive features like pop-up spells and hidden compartments, and include hidden messages using invisible ink, codes, and runes.

Enchanted Ink and Writing Tools: How to Create Your Own Magical Ink

The act of writing in your spellbook is a ritual in itself. Using enchanted ink and special writing tools imbues your entries with additional power and intention. Crafting your own magical ink can be a rewarding process, allowing you to select ingredients that align with specific energies and purposes.

1. Ingredients for Enchanted Ink

Creating magical ink involves using natural ingredients that correspond with your intention. Here are some common ingredients and their properties:

- **Herbs:**
    - **Rosemary:** Enhances clarity and protection.
    - **Lavender:** Invites peace and relaxation.
    - **Sage:** Purifies and wards off negativity.
    - **Mugwort:** Promotes intuition and dreamwork.
- **Essential Oils:**
    - **Frankincense:** Encourages spiritual connection.
    - **Rose:** Attracts love and beauty.
    - **Peppermint:** Sharpens focus and communication.
- **Base Liquid:**
    - **Water:** Distilled water is a neutral base for ink.

- ◦ **Moon Water:** Water charged under the moonlight, perfect for spells of intuition and healing.
- ◦ **Alcohol:** Adds fluidity and prevents mold growth; use vodka or grain alcohol for best results.
- ◦ **Vinegar:** Adds a slight acidity for aged-looking ink and works well with plant dyes.

2. Crafting Your Own Magical Ink

Here's a simple recipe for creating enchanted ink using common ingredients:

Ingredients:

- 1 tablespoon of dried herbs (e.g., rosemary, sage, or lavender)
- ½ cup distilled water or moon water
- 1 tablespoon vinegar (optional, for longevity)
- 3-5 drops of essential oil (e.g., frankincense, peppermint)
- A small jar with a lid
- A fine strainer or cheesecloth

Instructions:

1. **Create a Herbal Infusion:** Place the dried herbs in a small pot and add the distilled water or moon water. Bring the mixture to a simmer for 10-15 minutes, allowing the water to absorb the herb's essence. As it simmers, stir gently and focus on your intention for the ink.
2. **Strain the Mixture:** Remove the pot from heat and let it cool slightly. Strain the liquid into a small jar, separating the herbs from the liquid.
3. **Add Essential Oils:** Add 3-5 drops of essential oil that corresponds with your intention (e.g., frankincense for spiritual clarity). Stir gently, visualizing your energy infusing into the ink.

4. **Seal and Store:** Add a tablespoon of vinegar to the jar to preserve the ink. Seal the jar with a lid and store it in a cool, dark place. Shake well before each use.

3. Using Your Enchanted Ink

- **Writing Spells:** Use a dip pen or calligraphy brush to write spells, sigils, and runes in your spellbook. Enchanted ink adds a layer of energy to each word, enhancing the spell's power.
- **Color Correspondences:** To create inks of different colors, use natural dyes like beet juice (red), spinach juice (green), or blueberry juice (purple). Match the ink color to the type of spell (e.g., green for abundance, blue for tranquility).
- **Charging the Ink:** Place the ink under the full moon, in a circle of crystals, or next to a burning candle to charge it with additional energy before use.

Pop-Up Spells and Hidden Compartments: Adding Interactive Elements to Your Book

Adding interactive elements like pop-up spells and hidden compartments makes your spellbook not only visually intriguing but also magically potent. These features allow you to conceal secrets, store small items, and create a dynamic, hands-on experience when using your spellbook.

1. Creating Pop-Up Spells

Pop-up spells are three-dimensional pages that can be pulled, folded, or opened to reveal hidden symbols, sigils, or messages. Here's how to create a simple pop-up spell:

Materials:

- Heavyweight paper or cardstock
- Scissors
- Glue or double-sided tape

- Markers or paints for decoration

Instructions:

1. **Choose a Design:** Decide on the pop-up element for the spell, such as a pentacle, flower, or moon. Draw or trace the design onto the cardstock and cut it out.
2. **Create the Pop-Up Mechanism:** Cut two strips of cardstock (approximately 1 inch wide and 2 inches long). Fold each strip into an accordion shape to act as the pop-up hinges.
3. **Attach the Hinges:** Glue one end of each accordion hinge to the back of the cut-out design. Then, glue the other end of the hinges to the spellbook page where you want the pop-up to appear.
4. **Decorate the Page:** Use markers, paints, or stickers to decorate the surrounding page with symbols, words, or other elements related to the spell. When the page is opened, the pop-up design will spring forward, revealing the magical symbol.
5. **Add Correspondences:** You can write correspondences or instructions beneath the pop-up element, creating an interactive and layered experience.

2. Incorporating Hidden Compartments

Hidden compartments allow you to store small magical items, such as charms, herbs, crystals, or notes, directly in your spellbook.

How to Create a Hidden Compartment:

1. **Cut a Page Pocket:** Choose a thicker page near the back of your spellbook. Use a craft knife to cut along three sides of a rectangular area, leaving the top edge uncut. This creates a flap that can be lifted to reveal a pocket.
2. **Reinforce the Pocket:** Apply a thin line of glue along the inner edges of the cut rectangle (except for the top) and press another piece of paper over it to create a secure pocket.

3. **Decorate the Flap:** Draw symbols or add stickers to the flap to blend it with the page's design, camouflaging the compartment.

4. **Add Contents:** Place a small item, sigil, or piece of paper with a spell inside the pocket. Close the flap to keep it hidden.

3. Adding Interactive Flaps and Doors

- **Folded Flaps:** Glue small, folded pieces of paper onto the page to act as flaps that can be lifted to reveal hidden messages, symbols, or spells.
- **Mini Envelopes:** Attach tiny envelopes to the pages and fill them with notes, herbs, or tiny talismans. Seal them with a sticker or wax seal for an added layer of secrecy.
- **Hidden Symbols:** Create doors by cutting along the edges of a drawn symbol and folding it open to reveal additional information or images beneath.

Incorporating Hidden Messages: Using Invisible Ink, Codes, or Runes

Hidden messages add an extra layer of mystique and protection to your spellbook. By using invisible ink, codes, or runes, you can conceal private spells, notes, or insights that only you can decipher.

1. Writing with Invisible Ink

Invisible ink is a classic way to hide messages that can only be revealed under specific conditions, such as heat or UV light.

How to Make Invisible Ink:

- **Lemon Juice Method:** Squeeze fresh lemon juice into a small bowl. Use a fine-tipped brush or cotton swab to write your message on the paper. Once the juice dries, the writing will be invisible.

- **Revealing the Message:** To reveal the hidden writing, hold the page near a candle flame or light bulb (without letting it burn). The heat will darken the lemon juice, making the message visible.

Additional Methods:

- **Milk:** Milk can also be used as invisible ink. Write with milk and reveal the message by heating the paper.
- **Baking Soda Solution:** Mix a small amount of baking soda with water to create an invisible ink. Use grape juice to reveal the hidden writing; the juice will react with the baking soda, changing color where the message was written.

2. Creating Codes and Ciphers

Using codes and ciphers to encode your spells adds a layer of secrecy that only you or trusted individuals can understand.

- **Simple Substitution Cipher:** Replace each letter of your message with another letter or symbol. For example, you might shift each letter in the alphabet by three spaces (A becomes D, B becomes E) to create a basic cipher. Write the key in a hidden page of your spellbook for reference.
- **Runic Alphabets:** Use a runic alphabet, such as the Elder Futhark, to encode your spells. Replace each letter in your words with a corresponding rune. This not only adds secrecy but also infuses the writing with the energy of ancient runic magic.
- **Numerology:** Assign numbers to each letter (A=1, B=2, C=3, etc.) and write your messages in numeric form. Use a numerology chart in your spellbook to decode the messages later.

3. Creating Sigil Messages

- **Layered Sigils:** Create sigils that incorporate symbols, letters, or numbers representing your hidden message. Only you will know the true meaning encoded in the design. Use these sigils as protective seals, spell anchors, or secret markers within your spellbook.
- **Underpainted Symbols:** Paint a page with watercolors, and while it's still wet, draw your sigil or message lightly into the paint. As it dries, the sigil will become nearly invisible, only discernible to those who know how to look for it.

By incorporating enchanted ink, pop-up spells, hidden compartments, and coded messages, you transform your spellbook into a magical artifact filled with layers of mystique, energy, and personal meaning. These mystical elements not only enhance the visual and interactive qualities of your spellbook but also strengthen the magical bonds within its pages. As you continue to add these elements, your spellbook will grow into a powerful, unique tool that mirrors your magical journey and intentions.

Chapter 8: Personalizing the Spellbook

A spellbook is a deeply personal object, reflecting your journey, experiences, and growth as a magical practitioner. It's more than a repository of spells and correspondences; it's a unique diary of your spiritual and magical path. Personalizing your spellbook with photos, doodles, dream logs, tarot readings, seasonal spells, and notes infuses it with your energy and makes it a living, breathing document of your practice. This chapter will guide you on how to make your spellbook uniquely yours, ensuring it becomes a cherished tool in your magical workings.

Adding Personal Touches: Incorporating Photos, Doodles, and Notes

Personal touches can transform a spellbook from a mere reference guide into a magical artifact filled with your essence and energy. Adding photos, doodles, and handwritten notes allows you to embed your spellbook with memories, emotions, and intentions.

1. Incorporating Photos

- **Purpose:** Including photos in your spellbook adds a visual and emotional layer to your magical records. Use photos to document ritual setups, magical tools, natural elements, or events that have personal significance.
- **Ideas for Incorporating Photos:**
  - **Ritual Documentation:** Take photos of your altar setup, ritual tools, or spell components. Include these photos next to written entries describing the ritual's purpose, steps, and outcome.
  - **Nature Walks:** Include pictures from nature walks or visits to sacred sites, such as forests, rivers, mountains, or historical landmarks. Write notes about the energy of the

place, any intuitive insights you received, and how you
might use elements from the environment in your practice.

- ° **Spellcraft Artifacts:** Document artifacts you use or create
  in your magic, such as wands, pentacles, or crystals. For instance, you might include a photo of a homemade charm
  bag along with its ingredients and purpose.
- **Attachment Methods:** Use glue, double-sided tape, or photo
  corners to attach the images to the pages. If you prefer a more
  dynamic approach, consider adding pockets or envelopes to hold
  loose photos and notes.

2. Adding Doodles and Sketches

- **Purpose:** Doodles and sketches add a playful, whimsical touch to
  your spellbook, enhancing its visual appeal. Even simple drawings
  of symbols, plants, or mystical creatures can infuse the pages with
  creative energy.
- **Doodling Ideas:**
    - ° **Borders:** Draw vines, stars, moons, or spirals as borders
      around your spells, rituals, or correspondences to create a
      sense of enchantment on each page.
    - ° **Symbols:** Sketch magical symbols, such as pentacles,
      moons, runes, or alchemical glyphs, to enhance the mean-
      ing of each spell or entry.
    - ° **Herbs and Crystals:** Illustrate herbs, crystals, and other
      ingredients you frequently use in your practice. For exam-
      ple, draw a small lavender sprig next to spells that involve
      calm and relaxation, or sketch a crescent moon beside en-
      tries related to lunar magic.
- **Incorporating Color:** Use colored pens, pencils, or watercolors
  to make your sketches vibrant. Choose colors that correspond
  with the energy of the spell or ritual (e.g., green for prosperity,
  blue for tranquility).

3. Handwritten Notes and Affirmations

- **Journaling Your Thoughts:** Reserve a section of your spellbook for personal reflections, observations, and thoughts. Jot down your feelings before and after rituals, your dreams and aspirations, or any magical experiences you wish to remember.
- **Affirmations:** Write positive affirmations throughout your spellbook to maintain a positive energy flow. For example, include phrases like "I am powerful and in control of my destiny" or "The universe provides guidance and protection."
- **Quotations:** Add quotes from favorite authors, poets, or spiritual guides that resonate with your practice. Handwriting these quotes adds a personal touch and anchors their wisdom into your spellbook.

Magical Record Keeping: Including Dream Logs, Tarot Readings, and Spell Results

Keeping records of your magical experiences, dreams, and divination practices provides valuable insights and helps you track your spiritual progress. Including dream logs, tarot readings, and spell results in your spellbook not only adds depth but also serves as a personal archive of your magical journey.

1. Dream Logs

- **Purpose:** Dreams often contain messages from the subconscious, spirit guides, or the universe. Recording your dreams allows you to analyze recurring symbols, emotions, and themes, providing a deeper understanding of your inner self.
- **Setting Up a Dream Log:**
  - **Dream Details:** Include the date of each dream and a brief description of what happened. Record key symbols, feelings, colors, and characters that appeared in the dream.

- **Reflections:** Add a section for interpretations, insights, or questions that arise from the dream. Consider the dream's relevance to your current life, magical work, or spiritual path.
- **Recurring Themes:** Keep track of recurring symbols or themes over time. For example, if you repeatedly dream about water, you might explore its significance in your emotional state or magical practice.

• **Adding Illustrations:** Sketch symbols or scenes from your dreams to create a visual representation that captures their essence. This can help you connect more deeply with the dream's messages and energies.

2. Tarot and Divination Records

• **Purpose:** Documenting your tarot readings, rune casts, or other divination practices helps you track patterns, guidance, and insights you receive over time.
• **How to Record Tarot Readings:**
  - **Date and Spread:** Record the date of the reading and the tarot spread you used (e.g., three-card spread, Celtic Cross).
  - **Card Positions and Meanings:** Note the cards drawn and their positions within the spread. Write down their meanings and how they relate to your question or situation.
  - **Personal Reflections:** Include your interpretations, feelings, and any messages that come through during the reading. Reflect on how the cards' meanings might apply to your life or spellwork.
  - **Follow-Up:** Consider revisiting past readings to see how the guidance has unfolded. Write updates on events, lessons, or revelations that occurred since the reading.

- **Other Divination Methods:** Document other divination practices, such as rune casting, pendulum dowsing, scrying, or tea leaf reading. Include drawings of runes, scrying symbols, or pendulum charts alongside their interpretations.

3. Spell Results

- **Purpose:** Recording the results of your spells allows you to assess their effectiveness, refine your methods, and gain a deeper understanding of your magical process.
- **How to Track Spell Outcomes:**
    - **Spell Entry:** For each spell, include the date it was performed, the intention, the ingredients, and the steps you took.
    - **Observations:** Write down any immediate sensations, signs, or omens you experienced during or shortly after the spell. Include details such as candle flickering, crystal vibrations, or sudden emotional shifts.
    - **Results:** Document the spell's outcome, noting when and how the desired result manifested (or didn't). If the outcome was different from what you intended, reflect on possible reasons (e.g., timing, correspondences, or clarity of intention).
- **Adjustments:** Use these records to identify what worked well and what might need adjusting. This practice helps you hone your spellcraft and develop more effective techniques over time.

Seasonal Spells: Creating Special Pages for Halloween, Sabbats, and Other Holidays

The changing seasons, lunar cycles, and spiritual holidays offer potent times for magical work. Including seasonal spells in your spellbook allows you to align your practice with nature's rhythms and the energies of the earth. Here's how to create special pages for seasonal and holiday magic:

1. Celebrating Sabbats

Sabbats are the eight seasonal festivals that make up the Wiccan Wheel of the Year. Each Sabbat represents a unique point in the cycle of nature, reflecting the themes of the changing seasons. By dedicating a section of your spellbook to each Sabbat, you can document rituals, spells, correspondences, and personal reflections, aligning your practice with the Earth's rhythms. In this section, we will explore how to celebrate all eight Sabbats with spells, rituals, correspondences, and decorative elements.

1. Sabbat Entries

Dedicate a page or section of your spellbook to each Sabbat, including the date, symbols, colors, herbs, crystals, deities, and traditional correspondences. Use these entries to outline the unique energy and themes associated with each festival. Incorporate your own reflections, ideas for rituals, and ways you plan to celebrate.

2. Seasonal Spells for Each Sabbat

Here's a guide to the eight Sabbats, their themes, and ideas for spells and rituals to include in your spellbook.

Samhain (October 31)

- Themes: Death and rebirth, honoring ancestors, divination, transformation, introspection.
- Symbols: Pumpkins, skeletons, candles, apples, cauldrons.
- Correspondences:
    - Colors: Black, orange, deep purple.
    - Herbs: Mugwort, sage, rosemary, wormwood.
    - Crystals: Obsidian, onyx, amethyst.
    - Deities: Hecate, Cailleach, Morrigan, Anubis.
- Seasonal Spells:
    - Ancestor Honoring: Create a spell to honor your ancestors. Light a candle and place a photo or memento of a loved one on your altar. Say a few words of remembrance and gratitude.
    - Protection Spell: Craft a protection spell to guard your home during the dark half of the year. Use black candles, sage, and obsidian to create a protective barrier.
    - Divination: Perform a divination ritual using tarot cards, runes, or scrying to gain insights into the coming year. Record your findings in your spellbook.
- Decorative Elements: Press dried orange slices and place them on the page. Add drawings of pumpkins, cauldrons, or skulls. Use black and orange ink to write your spells and rituals.

Yule (Winter Solstice, around December 21)

- Themes: Renewal, rebirth of the sun, hope, warmth, light, introspection.
- Symbols: Holly, ivy, mistletoe, Yule log, candles, sun wheels.
- Correspondences:
    - Colors: Red, green, gold, white.
    - Herbs: Pine, cedar, cinnamon, cloves, frankincense.
    - Crystals: Clear quartz, garnet, bloodstone.
    - Deities: Sun gods (e.g., Apollo, Ra), Great Mother, Oak King, Holly King.
- Seasonal Spells:
    - Light and Warmth: Write a spell to invite light and warmth into your life. Light a candle, sprinkle it with cinnamon for prosperity, and chant words of renewal.
    - Manifesting New Intentions: Set your intentions for the new year. Create a list of goals and desires, and perform a candle spell using a gold candle to symbolize the returning light.
    - Yule Log Ritual: Decorate a Yule log with holly, pinecones, and ribbons. As you burn the log (or visualize burning it in your spellbook), release old energies and welcome new beginnings.
- Decorative Elements: Attach sprigs of holly or pine needles to the page. Draw symbols of the sun, stars, or candles. Use red and green ink with gold accents to highlight spells and rituals.

Imbolc (February 1-2)

- Themes: Purification, light returning, preparation, creativity, new beginnings.
- Symbols: Candles, snowdrops, Brigid's cross, hearth fires.
- Correspondences:
  - Colors: White, silver, yellow, light green.
  - Herbs: Basil, angelica, myrrh, lavender.
  - Crystals: Amethyst, garnet, onyx.
  - Deities: Brigid, Athena, Eros, Persephone.
- Seasonal Spells:
  - Purification Ritual: Create a cleansing ritual to purify your space and energy. Burn sage or lavender while visualizing stagnant energy being cleared away.
  - Candle Magic: Write a candle spell to symbolize the growing light. Use white candles for purity and yellow for inspiration. Add a chant to your spellbook that invokes creativity and warmth.
  - Brigid's Cross Crafting: Include instructions for making a Brigid's Cross from reeds or paper as a protective charm for your home.
- Decorative Elements: Decorate with drawings of snowdrops, flames, or Brigid's cross. Press dried lavender or sprinkle lavender buds on the page. Use silver and yellow ink to capture the essence of light and purity.

Ostara (Spring Equinox, around March 21)

- Themes: Balance, fertility, growth, renewal, planting seeds.
- Symbols: Eggs, rabbits, flowers, seeds.
- Correspondences:
    - Colors: Pastel pink, green, yellow, lavender.
    - Herbs: Daffodil, jasmine, violets, lilac.
    - Crystals: Rose quartz, moonstone, aquamarine.
    - Deities: Eostre, Demeter, Persephone, Pan.
- Seasonal Spells:
    - Growth and Fertility: Write a spell to encourage personal growth or fertility in projects. Include symbols of eggs or seeds and use green candles for abundance.
    - Egg Magic: Include a spell using colored eggs. Write your desires or goals on the eggshell, then bury it in the ground to symbolize planting the seeds of your intentions.
    - Balance Ritual: Create a ritual for inner balance using an equal-armed cross symbol or drawing the scales. Light candles of opposing colors (e.g., black and white) to represent harmony.
- Decorative Elements: Draw flowers, rabbits, and eggs to adorn the pages. Attach pressed flowers or flower petals for a fresh, vibrant touch. Use pastel colors for writing to reflect the light and growth of spring.

Beltane (May 1)

- Themes: Fertility, passion, love, vitality, blossoming.
- Symbols: Maypole, flowers, ribbons, bonfires.
- Correspondences:
    - Colors: Red, pink, green, white.
    - Herbs: Hawthorn, rose, lilac, thyme.
    - Crystals: Emerald, rose quartz, garnet.
    - Deities: Flora, Pan, Aphrodite, Cernunnos.
- Seasonal Spells:
    - Love Spell: Write a spell for self-love or romantic attraction using rose petals, rose quartz, and pink candles. Include words of affirmation and passion.
    - Bonfire Ritual: Describe how to create a mini bonfire (or candle flame) ritual in your spellbook to ignite the fires of creativity and passion.
    - Abundance Charm: Craft a charm bag with green herbs, flowers, and a piece of citrine to attract abundance. Include the instructions and incantation in your spellbook.
- Decorative Elements: Press flowers, such as roses and lilacs, onto the pages. Draw symbols like the Maypole, ribbons, and flower wreaths. Write with red, pink, and green ink to capture the vitality and passion of Beltane.

Litha (Summer Solstice, around June 21)

- Themes: Power, energy, abundance, light, strength.
- Symbols: Sun wheels, sunflowers, oak leaves, fire.
- Correspondences:
  - Colors: Gold, yellow, green, blue.
  - Herbs: St. John's wort, chamomile, lavender, vervain.
  - Crystals: Sunstone, amber, clear quartz.
  - Deities: Sun gods (e.g., Ra, Apollo), Gaia, Aine, Lugh.
- Seasonal Spells:
  - Sunlight Spell: Create a spell to harness the power of the sun. Write a chant that invokes strength, vitality, and success, using a piece of sunstone as a focal point.
  - Solar Energy Ritual: Design a ritual for charging crystals or magical tools in the sunlight. Include instructions for placing items in the sun and visualizing them absorbing solar energy.
  - Abundance Jar: Write a spell for creating an abundance jar. Fill a small jar with sunflowers, cinnamon, and gold coins, sealing it with golden wax while chanting words of prosperity.
- Decorative Elements: Add drawings of the sun, sunflowers, and flames. Use dried sunflower petals or oak leaves to enhance the page. Write with gold or yellow ink to represent the sun's energy.

Lammas (Lughnasadh, August 1)

- Themes: Harvest, abundance, gratitude, sacrifice, preparation.
- Symbols: Wheat, corn, bread, sickles.
- Correspondences:
    - Colors: Gold, yellow, orange, brown.
    - Herbs: Wheat, barley, corn, heather.
    - Crystals: Citrine, tiger's eye, carnelian.
    - Deities: Lugh, Demeter, Ceres, Thor.
- Seasonal Spells:
    - Gratitude Ritual: Write a ritual to give thanks for the harvest in your life. Light a yellow candle and list the things you are grateful for on a piece of parchment. Burn the paper as an offering.
    - Prosperity Bread Spell: Include a spell for baking bread infused with intentions of prosperity and abundance. Describe how to bless the dough and visualize the bread rising with your desires.
    - Harvest Jar: Create a spell for making a harvest jar filled with grains, herbs, and small notes of gratitude. Seal the jar with a golden ribbon.
- Decorative Elements: Draw images of wheat sheaves, bread, and sickles. Attach dried wheat stalks or corn husks to the page. Use orange, gold, and brown ink to reflect the colors of the harvest.

Mabon (Autumn Equinox, around September 21)

- Themes: Balance, gratitude, harvest, preparation, reflection.
- Symbols: Apples, leaves, cornucopia, pumpkins.
- Correspondences:
  - Colors: Red, orange, yellow, brown.
  - Herbs: Apple, sage, oak leaves, rosemary.
  - Crystals: Citrine, jasper, smoky quartz.
  - Deities: Demeter, Persephone, Mabon, Thor.
- Seasonal Spells:
  - Balance Ritual: Write a ritual to bring balance into your life. Use two candles (one black, one white) to symbolize light and dark. Include a chant for harmony and equilibrium.
  - Gratitude Journal: Create a gratitude journaling spell. List things you are grateful for and how you will prepare for the darker half of the year.
  - Apple Blessing: Include a spell for blessing apples as symbols of abundance and protection. Describe how to cut the apple crosswise to reveal the pentacle and chant words of blessing over it.
- Decorative Elements: Draw autumn leaves, apples, and pumpkins. Use pressed oak leaves or apple slices for decoration. Write in shades of red, orange, and brown to evoke the warmth of autumn.

By creating detailed pages for each Sabbat in your spellbook, you establish a connection to the natural world and its cycles. This practice not only enriches your magical workings but also aligns your energy with the rhythm of the Earth. As the Wheel of the Year turns, your spellbook will serve as a guide, reminding you of the unique magic each season holds.

2. Lunar and Solar Festivals

- **Full Moon Spells:** Create pages dedicated to different full moons throughout the year (e.g., Harvest Moon, Hunter's Moon, Wolf Moon). Write spells that correspond with each moon's energy, such as abundance, release, intuition, or transformation.
- **New Moon Rituals:** Reserve space for new moon rituals that focus on setting intentions, new beginnings, and manifestation. Include a list of new moon affirmations or journaling prompts to explore your goals and desires.
- **Solar Events:** Document solar events like the equinoxes and solstices. Include rituals for balance, gratitude, or welcoming the shift in energy that comes with each change of season.

3. Holiday Magic

The Wheel of the Year is not the only opportunity to infuse magic into your practice; traditional holidays, both spiritual and secular, offer additional occasions to celebrate and work with unique energies. By dedicating sections of your spellbook to these holidays, you can craft spells and rituals that align with the energies they bring. This part of your spellbook becomes a chronicle of celebrations, creating a record of magical traditions that grow and evolve with each year. Here, we explore ways to incorporate magic into Halloween, Yule (Christmas), Valentine's Day, and other major holidays.

1. Halloween Magic (Samhain, October 31)

Halloween, or Samhain, is a time when the veil between worlds is thin, making it a potent period for divination, spirit communication, and protection. This holiday marks the end of the harvest season and the beginning of winter, symbolizing both death and rebirth.

- Samhain Entries: In your spellbook, detail the history and significance of Halloween/Samhain. Include correspondences such as colors (black, orange, purple), symbols (pumpkins, bats, skulls), herbs (mugwort, sage, rosemary), and crystals (obsidian, onyx, amethyst).
- Spells and Rituals:
    - Divination: Document tarot, rune, or pendulum readings performed on Halloween night. Write down any messages or visions received, as this is a time when insights from the otherworld are particularly strong.

- ◦ Spirit Communication: Create a spell for safely connecting with ancestors and spirit guides. Light candles on your altar and place photos or mementos of loved ones. Include instructions for using a black mirror or scrying bowl for spirit communication.
- ◦ Protection Spell: Write a protection spell to shield your home and loved ones during this time. Use black candles, salt, and protective crystals like obsidian. Include a chant or incantation to invoke protective energies.
- ◦ Ancestor Ritual: Add a ritual for honoring the ancestors, involving lighting a candle and setting out food or drink offerings. Note any intuitive impressions or messages you receive during the ritual.
- Decorative Elements: Use pressed leaves, dried orange slices, or cinnamon sticks to decorate the page. Draw symbols like pumpkins, bats, moons, and skeletons. Use black, orange, and deep purple ink to match the season's colors.

2. Yule (Christmas, Winter Solstice, around December 21)

Yule, celebrated around the Winter Solstice, marks the rebirth of the sun and the return of the light. It is a time for renewal, reflection, and celebrating the warmth of family and friends.

- Yule Entries: Write about the customs and folklore of Yule and Christmas, noting correspondences such as colors (red, green, gold, white), symbols (holly, ivy, candles, sun wheels), herbs (pine, cinnamon, frankincense), and crystals (clear quartz, garnet, bloodstone).
- Spells and Rituals:
    ◦ Renewal Spell: Create a spell to release the old and welcome the new. Light a white candle and meditate on what you wish to let go of from the past year. Write your desires for the upcoming year on a piece of paper, then fold it and place it under the candle to charge it with intention.
    ◦ Yule Log Ritual: Describe how to create a Yule log ritual in your spellbook. Decorate a log with evergreen branches, holly, and ribbons, then burn it in a fireplace or a cauldron to symbolize the sun's return.
    ◦ Manifestation Jar: Write instructions for a manifestation jar spell to attract abundance and joy in the coming year. Fill the jar with herbs like cinnamon, clove, and orange peel, along with symbols of wealth (coins, sunstones).
    ◦ Altar Decorations: Document how to decorate your altar for Yule with evergreens, pinecones, candles, and sun symbols. Include a short ritual for lighting candles on the solstice night to honor the rebirth of the sun.
- Decorative Elements: Use pressed holly leaves or pine needles to adorn the page. Draw candles, stars, and snowflakes. Write with red, green, and gold ink to reflect the festive energy of the season.

3. Valentine's Day (February 14)

Valentine's Day is associated with love, romance, and affection. This holiday's energy can be harnessed not only for romantic love but also for self-love, friendship, and harmony in relationships.

- Valentine's Day Entries: Include correspondences such as colors (pink, red, white), symbols (hearts, roses, Cupid, doves), herbs (rose, lavender, jasmine), and crystals (rose quartz, amethyst, garnet).
- Spells and Rituals:
  - Self-Love Ritual: Write a ritual for self-love using rose petals, a pink candle, and rose quartz. Include affirmations like "I am worthy of love and respect" and steps for a self-care bath or beauty ritual.
  - Love Spell: Create a simple love spell using a red or pink candle, a drop of rose essential oil, and a rose petal. Include words of intention to attract love into your life or strengthen an existing relationship.
  - Friendship Harmony Spell: Describe a spell to enhance friendship using lavender, a purple candle, and a piece of amethyst. Write down how to use a photo or memento representing your friendship as a focal point during the ritual.
  - Love Potion: Include a recipe for a Valentine's Day love potion made with ingredients like rose water, honey, and a splash of pomegranate juice. Write instructions on how to use the potion as a magical beverage to attract love or promote self-love.
- Decorative Elements: Use dried rose petals, pressed flower petals, or small ribbons to embellish the page. Draw hearts, doves, and

flowers. Use red and pink ink to enhance the theme of love and affection.

4. Easter (Ostara, Spring Equinox, around March 21)

Easter, closely aligned with the Wiccan Sabbat Ostara, celebrates the themes of rebirth, fertility, and renewal. It's a time for planting seeds, both physically and metaphorically.

- Easter Entries: Include correspondences such as colors (pastel pink, green, yellow), symbols (eggs, bunnies, flowers), herbs (daffodil, jasmine, lilac), and crystals (rose quartz, moonstone, aquamarine).
- Spells and Rituals:
  - Egg Magic: Describe an egg charm spell where you write your wishes on eggshells, then bury them in the earth as a symbolic planting of your intentions.
  - Renewal Ritual: Write a ritual for spring renewal, involving the lighting of a green candle and the planting of seeds. Document steps to bless the seeds with growth and prosperity.
  - Flower Crown Ritual: Create a spell using a handmade flower crown. Include instructions for weaving the crown with fresh flowers and herbs, imbuing it with intentions for beauty, fertility, and creativity.
- Decorative Elements: Attach pressed flower petals or dried grass to the page. Draw symbols like eggs, rabbits, and budding flowers. Use pastel colors for writing to capture the energy of spring.

5. **Midsummer (June 24)**

Midsummer, or St. John's Day, celebrates the height of summer, solar power, and the abundance of the earth.

- Midsummer Entries: Include correspondences such as colors (yellow, gold, blue), symbols (sun, fire, herbs), herbs (St. John's Wort, chamomile, lavender), and crystals (citrine, amber, sunstone).
- Spells and Rituals:
    - Sun Blessing: Document a ritual to honor the sun's power. Write about how to use sun-charged water in spells or to bless your tools.
    - Fire Magic: Include a spell for burning herbs like rosemary, lavender, or sage in a bonfire or candle flame to release wishes into the universe.
- Decorative Elements: Draw the sun, flames, and sunflowers. Use dried herbs and bright yellow or gold ink to highlight the energy of midsummer.

6. **Halloween (October 31)**

Already covered in detail above, Halloween is synonymous with magic, mystery, and celebrating the spirit world.

7. **Thanksgiving (Fourth Thursday in November)**

Thanksgiving is a time for gratitude, abundance, and the harvest. It's an opportunity to reflect on the blessings in your life and express thanks to the universe.

- Thanksgiving Entries: Include correspondences such as colors (brown, orange, yellow, red), symbols (cornucopia, pumpkins, wheat), herbs (sage, thyme, rosemary), and crystals (citrine, carnelian, garnet).
- Spells and Rituals:
    - Gratitude Spell: Write a spell of gratitude using a yellow candle, a piece of paper, and a pen. Note down things you are thankful for and place the paper beneath the candle. Light the candle and give thanks to the universe.
    - Cornucopia Charm: Describe how to create a cornucopia charm filled with symbols of abundance (dried corn, wheat, coins) to place on your altar.
- Decorative Elements: Attach dried wheat or corn husks to the page. Draw symbols like pumpkins, turkeys, and cornucopias. Use orange, brown, and red ink to capture the warmth of the season.

By incorporating pages for each holiday into your spellbook, you align your practice with the ebb and flow of both the natural world and cultural celebrations. Each section becomes a ritual in itself, filled with spells, correspondences, decorations, and reflections that make your spellbook a true testament to the magic of everyday life.

4. Designing Seasonal Pages

- **Colors and Themes:** Use colors that align with each season or holiday. For example, use deep oranges, purples, and blacks for Halloween spells, or pastel pinks, greens, and yellows for spring and Beltane.
- **Artistic Elements:** Include drawings, watercolor backgrounds, or stickers that represent the season's essence. For a Halloween page, draw pumpkins, bats, and moon phases; for a Yule page, sketch holly, pine cones, and candles.
- **Herbs and Incense:** Note the herbs, spices, and incense associated with each season or holiday. For example, list cinnamon, clove, and frankincense for Yule, or rosemary and sage for Samhain.

By personalizing your spellbook with photos, doodles, magical records, and seasonal spells, you create a truly unique and evolving magical tool. Each entry, sketch, and note becomes a piece of your journey, infusing the spellbook with your energy, intentions, and experiences. As you add more personal elements, your spellbook transforms into a living testament to your path and practice, growing and evolving alongside you.

Chapter 9: Caring for Your Spellbook

Your spellbook is a powerful tool filled with your energy, intentions, and magical knowledge. Caring for it properly ensures that it remains a potent and enduring part of your practice. This chapter provides guidance on how to store, cleanse, recharge, and update your spellbook to preserve its energy and keep it aligned with your evolving magical journey.

Storing the Spellbook: Tips for Keeping It Safe and Preserved

Proper storage is essential to protect your spellbook from physical damage and to preserve the energy it contains. Where and how you store your spellbook can influence its longevity and the strength of the magic within its pages.

1. Choosing a Safe Storage Location

- **Sacred Space:** Store your spellbook in a sacred space, such as an altar, a dedicated bookshelf, or a special drawer. Keeping it in an area that is already imbued with positive and protective energies helps maintain the book's magical potency.
- **Avoid High Traffic Areas:** Place your spellbook in a location that is not frequently disturbed. This minimizes the risk of damage and prevents unwanted energies from interfering with its contents. If you share your living space, store your spellbook somewhere private to maintain its secrecy and personal energy.
- **Protection:** Consider wrapping your spellbook in a cloth, such as silk, velvet, or cotton. Black cloths are ideal for absorbing and deflecting negative energy, while white cloths can purify and protect. You can also place the spellbook inside a wooden or fabric-lined box for added protection.

2. Environmental Considerations

- **Temperature and Humidity:** Store your spellbook in a cool, dry place away from direct sunlight, which can fade ink and weaken paper over time. Avoid humid environments, as moisture can cause pages to warp, stick together, or grow mold.
- **Avoid Extreme Conditions:** Keep your spellbook away from extreme conditions, such as near heaters, open flames, or in areas prone to water damage. Extreme heat can dry out the cover material, while water exposure can ruin the pages.
- **Pest Prevention:** To prevent damage from pests, consider placing herbs like dried lavender, cedar chips, or bay leaves near your spellbook. These natural repellents deter insects without introducing harsh chemicals that could harm the book.

3. Energy Protection

- **Crystal Guardians:** Place protective crystals, such as black tourmaline, obsidian, or clear quartz, near your spellbook. These stones help shield the book from negative energy and unwanted interference.
- **Warding Symbols:** Draw protective symbols or sigils on the storage container or wrap to create an energetic barrier around your spellbook. For example, a pentacle or a binding rune can serve as a protective ward.

Recharging and Cleansing: Rituals for Recharging the Book's Energy

Just as tools and crystals need regular cleansing and recharging, your spellbook also benefits from periodic energetic maintenance. Recharging and cleansing rituals help to refresh the book's energy, remove stagnation, and align it with your current magical intentions.

1. Cleansing Your Spellbook

- **Smudging:** Use smoke from cleansing herbs like sage, palo santo, rosemary, or lavender to purify your spellbook. Hold the book over the smoke, allowing it to drift over the cover and around the edges. While smudging, state your intention to clear away negative or stagnant energy, saying, "I cleanse this book of all negativity and stagnation. Only love, wisdom, and truth may reside within these pages."

- **Sound Cleansing:** Use a bell, chime, or singing bowl to cleanse your spellbook's energy. Place the book on your altar, and ring the bell or chime around it, focusing on the vibrations clearing away any negativity or blockages. Sound cleansing is gentle and effective, especially if you prefer not to use smoke.

- **Salt Circle:** For a more potent cleansing, create a circle of salt around your spellbook and leave it there for 24 hours. Salt is a natural purifier that absorbs negative energies. Afterward, dispose of the salt by burying it or washing it away with water.

2. Recharging Your Spellbook

- **Moonlight Charging:** Place your spellbook in the light of the full moon overnight to recharge its energy. The moon's energy infuses the book with intuitive, cleansing, and renewing vibrations. If you prefer to charge it during a specific moon phase (e.g., new moon for new beginnings, full moon for manifesting intentions), adjust accordingly.

- **Crystal Charging:** Place your spellbook on a bed of crystals that align with its purpose. Clear quartz amplifies the book's energy, rose quartz infuses it with love, and amethyst enhances spiritual insight. Allow the spellbook to rest on the crystals for several hours or overnight.

- **Candle Ritual:** Use candle magic to recharge your spellbook. Light a candle in a color that corresponds with your intention (e.g., white for purity, green for growth, purple for spiritual insight). Pass the book over the candle flame (carefully and at a safe distance) while visualizing the light filling the book with renewed energy. State an affirmation, such as, "I recharge this spellbook with the energy of light, love, and truth."

3. Personal Energy Recharging

- **Touch and Meditation:** Spend time holding your spellbook, running your fingers over the pages, and connecting with its energy. Close your eyes and breathe deeply, visualizing your personal energy merging with the book's essence. This practice not only recharges the spellbook but also strengthens your bond with it.

- **Anointing:** Anoint the cover or spine of your spellbook with a few drops of essential oil, such as lavender, frankincense, or rosemary. Choose an oil that aligns with the energy you wish to imbue into the book. This ritual helps to refresh its energy and connect it with your current intentions.

Updating the Book: Adding New Spells, Notes, and Information Over Time

Your spellbook is a living document that evolves with your practice. Regularly updating it with new spells, notes, and reflections keeps it relevant and aligned with your ongoing spiritual journey.

1. Adding New Spells and Rituals

- **New Moon Additions:** Use the new moon as a time to add new spells, rituals, and correspondences to your spellbook. The energy of new beginnings makes it an ideal period to introduce fresh magic into your practice.
- **Seasonal Updates:** Add information about Sabbats, seasonal correspondences, and holiday magic throughout the year. Include seasonal spells, altar setups, and reflections on how the changing seasons affect your practice. For example, document how you feel during each season and note any shifts in energy that influence your magic.
- **Current Projects:** Dedicate pages to ongoing magical projects, such as manifesting intentions, divination practices, or long-term rituals. Write down your progress, observations, and any insights gained along the way.

2. Revising and Reflecting

- **Review Past Spells:** Revisit spells and rituals you've previously recorded. Add notes about their outcomes, effectiveness, and any changes you made to the process. Reflecting on past work helps you refine your practice and recognize patterns in your magical journey.
- **Incorporate Learnings:** As you study and learn more about different magical systems, herbs, crystals, and correspondences, update your spellbook with this new information. Include foot-

notes or side notes in existing entries to expand on your knowledge and enhance the depth of your spells.

- **Rewrite or Remove Entries:** Don't be afraid to rewrite spells, rituals, or correspondences as your understanding deepens. If a spell no longer resonates with you or aligns with your current practice, you can cross it out (leaving it as a reminder of your growth) or remove it altogether in a respectful manner, such as burning or burying the page.

3. Personal Reflections and Notes

- **Dream Logs:** Add new dream entries and interpretations regularly. Over time, you may notice recurring symbols, themes, or messages that provide deeper insights into your subconscious and spiritual growth.
- **Tarot and Divination Records:** Update your divination sections with recent tarot readings, rune casts, or other forms of divination. Reflect on how these insights have played out and add new interpretations or questions that arise.
- **Affirmations and Intentions:** Write down new affirmations and intentions in your spellbook. As you set new goals or focus on different areas of your life, these entries help align the book's energy with your current path.

4. Enhancing Your Spellbook's Appearance

- **Artwork and Decorations:** As your practice grows, add new doodles, illustrations, stickers, pressed flowers, and other decorations to your spellbook. Personalizing its pages keeps it lively and visually engaging, inspiring you to continue working with it.
- **Tab Creation:** If your spellbook is expanding, consider adding tabs or dividers to help organize sections for easy access. Label

these tabs according to their contents, such as "Herbal Magic," "Moon Phases," "Spells & Rituals," and "Divination Records."

- **Magical Additions:** Include interactive elements, such as fold-out pages, pockets, or hidden compartments, as described in previous chapters. Adding new mystical elements over time keeps your spellbook dynamic and ever-evolving.

5. Seasonal Cleansing and Charging

- **Annual Cleanse:** Perform an annual cleansing and recharging ritual for your spellbook, preferably at a significant time, such as Samhain (the Wiccan New Year) or during a full moon. This ritual allows you to reflect on the past year's practices, clear away residual energies, and prepare your spellbook for the new cycle.
- **Dedicated Blessing:** Consider re-blessing your spellbook during a Sabbat or a personal milestone in your practice. Light candles, surround the book with crystals, and chant an incantation to renew its energy and power.

Caring for your spellbook involves more than just physical upkeep; it includes the rituals, energies, and personal attention you give to it. By storing it safely, regularly cleansing and recharging its energy, and updating its contents over time, you honor the spellbook as a sacred vessel for your magical journey. This ongoing care ensures that it remains a source of inspiration, wisdom, and power for years to come.

Chapter 10: Advanced Crafting Techniques

Incorporating advanced crafting techniques into your spellbook elevates it from a simple notebook to a personalized, magical artifact. Whether you aim to give it an antique appearance, add elegant binding elements, or adorn it with shimmering gold leaf, these techniques infuse your spellbook with deeper layers of beauty, intention, and power. This chapter will guide you through the process of aging pages, adding intricate bindings, and using embossing and gilding to make your spellbook a true masterpiece.

Aging the Pages: How to Create an Antique Look Using Tea Staining and Burning Edges

An aged, antique look can add a sense of mystery and wisdom to your spellbook, giving it the appearance of an ancient grimoire filled with age-old knowledge. The process of aging pages using tea staining and burning edges is straightforward and adds a vintage, worn character to the book's contents.

1. Tea Staining for an Antique Effect

Tea staining is a simple yet effective method for creating a weathered, yellowed look on the pages of your spellbook, reminiscent of old manuscripts.

Materials Needed:

- Black or green tea bags (black tea works best for a darker stain)
- Hot water
- A large bowl or shallow tray
- Paper towels
- Sponge or paintbrush (optional)
- Hair dryer (optional, for faster drying)

Instructions:

1. **Prepare the Tea:** Boil water and pour it into a bowl or shallow tray. Add 2-3 tea bags to the hot water and let them steep for at least 5-10 minutes. The longer the tea steeps, the darker the stain will be.
2. **Staining the Pages:** Carefully dip individual pages of your spellbook into the tea mixture, ensuring they are fully saturated. If you prefer not to immerse the entire page, use a sponge or paintbrush to dab the tea onto the paper. For a more uneven, aged look, concentrate the tea in certain areas and let it naturally spread.
3. **Creating Texture:** To add texture and visual interest, crumple the pages slightly while they are still wet, then smooth them out again. This technique gives the paper a worn, creased appearance.
4. **Drying the Pages:** Lay the pages flat on paper towels to air dry. If you wish to speed up the process, use a hair dryer on a low setting. As the pages dry, they will develop a natural yellowish hue and an aged texture.
5. **Sealing the Pages:** Once dry, consider lightly brushing the pages with a matte sealant or fixative spray to protect the tea stain and prevent the paper from becoming too brittle.

Tips for Variation:

- **Additional Stains:** For a more diverse aged effect, try staining some areas of the pages with coffee or red wine for varied color tones.
- **Ink Blots:** Add ink blots or splatters with a brush for an even older, well-used appearance.

2. Burning Edges for a Weathered Look

Burning the edges of the pages adds an element of mystery and drama, making the spellbook appear as though it has withstood time and various magical workings.

Materials Needed:

- A candle or lighter
- A bowl of water (for safety)
- Tweezers or tongs
- Fireproof surface

Instructions:

1. **Set Up a Safe Workspace:** Work in a well-ventilated area and on a fireproof surface. Have a bowl of water nearby in case of emergencies.
2. **Burn the Edges:** Hold a single page with tweezers and bring the edge close to a candle flame or lighter. Allow the flame to singe the edges lightly. Move the page along the flame, controlling the burn to create an uneven, natural look. Extinguish any flames quickly by blowing them out or dipping the page into water if necessary.
3. **Final Touches:** Gently tear parts of the burned edge with your fingers to create a tattered effect. Brush off the ash and loose bits from the edges.
4. **Protection:** If you plan to burn multiple pages, allow them to cool and settle before stacking them to avoid smudging. Once you have achieved the desired effect, apply a fixative spray to keep the burnt edges intact.

Tips for Variation:

- **Singed Patterns:** Lightly touch the middle of a page with the flame to create burn patterns, such as a scorched sigil or symbol, for an added magical element.
- **Combined Techniques:** Combine tea staining with burned edges to enhance the aged appearance, giving the pages a rich, historical look.

Binding Techniques: Adding Ribbon Bookmarks, Tassels, and Lock Clasps

The way you bind and embellish your spellbook's cover and spine not only enhances its appearance but also provides functional elements, like bookmarks and closures, to keep its pages safe and accessible.

1. Ribbon Bookmarks for Elegance and Functionality

Adding ribbon bookmarks to your spellbook allows you to easily mark significant sections while adding a decorative flair.

Materials Needed:

- Ribbons (in colors that correspond with your magical intentions)
- Needle and thread or fabric glue
- Scissors

Instructions:

1. **Select Ribbons:** Choose ribbons in various widths and colors that align with your spellbook's themes. For example, use black for protection, red for passion, or blue for tranquility.
2. **Measure and Cut:** Measure the height of your spellbook's spine and cut the ribbons to be approximately 1-2 inches longer than the book's height.

3. **Attach to the Spine:** If your spellbook has a softcover or flexible spine, you can sew the ribbons directly onto the inside of the spine using a needle and thread. Alternatively, use fabric glue to secure the ribbons to the top edge of the spine. Ensure the ribbons hang freely from the book.
4. **Finishing Touches:** For a decorative effect, tie small charms, beads, or crystals to the ends of the ribbons, infusing them with additional magical energy.

2. Tassels for a Mystical Touch

Tassels add an enchanting and tactile element to your spellbook's design.

Materials Needed:

- Embroidery thread or thin yarn
- Scissors
- Small piece of cardboard (to create uniform tassels)

Instructions:

1. **Wrap the Thread:** Wrap the embroidery thread around the cardboard multiple times to create the bulk of the tassel. The more times you wrap, the fuller the tassel will be.
2. **Create the Tassel:** Slide the wrapped thread off the cardboard and tie a piece of thread around the top to secure it. Cut the bottom loops to form the tassel's fringe.
3. **Attach to the Book:** Use thread or fabric glue to attach the tassel to the ribbon bookmarks or the top corner of the book's spine.
4. **Decorative Elements:** Add small charms, beads, or crystals to the tassel's top for an added magical touch.

3. Adding Lock Clasps for Secrecy and Protection

A lock clasp not only serves as a protective closure for your spellbook but also symbolizes the sealing of its magical knowledge.

Materials Needed:

- Lock clasp kit (available at craft stores)
- Screwdriver or glue
- Small lock and key (optional)

Instructions:

1. **Position the Clasp:** Determine the placement of the clasp on the front cover and spine or the front and back covers if you prefer a wraparound clasp. Mark the position with a pencil.
2. **Attach the Clasp:** If your kit includes screws, use a screwdriver to attach the clasp. If using glue, apply a small amount to the clasp's back and press it firmly onto the cover. Allow the glue to dry completely.
3. **Optional Lock:** If your clasp kit includes a small lock, use it to secure the clasp. Keep the key in a special place, such as on your altar or in a drawer dedicated to magical tools.
4. **Charging the Clasp:** Before using the clasp, perform a short ritual to charge it with protective energy. Hold your hand over the clasp and say, "This clasp seals my knowledge and guards my secrets. By my will, it is done."

Embossing and Gilding: Techniques for Adding Gold Leaf, Foiling, and Embossed Designs

Embossing and gilding add luxurious and mystical elements to your spellbook, turning it into a truly magical artifact. Embossed symbols provide texture and depth, while gilding adds a touch of gold or metallic shimmer to the cover or pages.

1. Embossing Designs for a Textured Effect

Embossing creates raised designs on your spellbook's cover, giving it an elegant and professional look.

Materials Needed:

- Embossing stamps or stencils
- Embossing ink pad
- Embossing powder (in desired colors)
- Heat gun
- Soft brush

Instructions:

1. **Choose a Design:** Select stamps or stencils with magical symbols, such as pentacles, runes, or sigils. If using a stencil, secure it in place with tape.
2. **Apply Embossing Ink:** Press the stamp onto the embossing ink pad and then onto the cover of your spellbook. If using a stencil, apply the ink over the stencil using a sponge.
3. **Sprinkle Embossing Powder:** Immediately sprinkle embossing powder over the inked area. Use a soft brush to remove excess powder and ensure the design is fully covered.

4. **Heat the Powder:** Use a heat gun to melt the embossing powder, creating a raised, glossy design. Move the heat gun slowly over the design until the powder melts and sets.

5. **Seal the Design:** Once the embossing has cooled, brush off any remaining powder and consider applying a clear sealant to protect the embossed design.

2. Gilding with Gold Leaf for a Luxurious Finish

Gilding adds metallic accents to your spellbook, giving it the appearance of ancient tomes adorned with gold.

Materials Needed:

- Gold leaf sheets (or metallic foil)
- Adhesive size (gilding glue)
- Soft brush
- Sealing varnish (optional)

Instructions:

1. **Apply Adhesive:** Using a soft brush, apply a thin layer of adhesive size to the areas where you want to apply gold leaf, such as symbols, edges, or lettering. Let the adhesive become tacky (usually takes a few minutes).

2. **Place the Gold Leaf:** Gently place a sheet of gold leaf over the adhesive. Use a soft brush to smooth the gold leaf onto the surface, pressing it into the design.

3. **Remove Excess Leaf:** Carefully brush away any excess gold leaf that does not adhere to the adhesive, revealing your gilded design.

4. **Seal the Gold Leaf:** To protect the gold leaf from tarnishing or rubbing off, apply a thin layer of sealing varnish once the gold leaf is fully set.

3. Foiling for a Modern Shimmer

If gold leaf seems too delicate, metallic foil provides a modern, sturdy alternative for adding shiny accents.

Materials Needed:

- Foiling sheets (in gold, silver, or other metallic colors)
- Foil adhesive
- Soft cloth or brush

Instructions:

1. **Apply Foil Adhesive:** Use a fine-tipped brush to apply foil adhesive in desired designs or lettering on the spellbook's cover or spine. Allow the adhesive to become tacky.
2. **Apply Foil:** Place the foil sheet, shiny side up, over the tacky adhesive. Use a soft cloth or brush to press the foil onto the adhesive, rubbing gently to transfer the foil to the surface.
3. **Reveal the Foil Design:** Slowly peel away the foil sheet, leaving the metallic design adhered to the book's surface. Brush off any loose foil fragments.
4. **Seal (Optional):** If desired, apply a clear sealant to protect the foiled areas from wear.

By employing these advanced crafting techniques—whether it's aging the pages, adding intricate bindings, or embossing and gilding the cover—you can transform your spellbook into a unique, beautiful artifact that reflects your personal magic. Each element you add not only enhances the book's appearance but also imbues it with intention, making it a powerful tool for your ongoing practice.

Appendices

Appendix A: Sample Spells and Rituals: Examples to Inspire Your Own Crafting

A spellbook is a collection of carefully crafted spells and rituals that capture the essence of your personal magic. It contains not just knowledge but also the creative expressions of your spiritual path. This appendix provides sample spells and rituals across various magical practices to inspire your own crafting. Each example includes detailed instructions, ingredients, and customizable elements, making them versatile templates for your own magical workings.

1. Protection Spell: Ward of the Four Elements

Purpose: To create a protective barrier around your space, infused with the power of the four elements (Earth, Air, Fire, and Water).

Ingredients:

- A bowl of salt (Earth)
- A feather (Air)
- A candle (Fire)
- A bowl of water (Water)
- Four small stones or crystals (e.g., obsidian, quartz)
- A small piece of paper and pen

Instructions:

1. **Set Up the Altar:** Arrange the elements on your altar or a flat surface. Place the bowl of salt in the north, the feather in the east, the candle in the south, and the bowl of water in the west. Position the four stones in a circle around these items.
2. **Write Your Intention:** On the piece of paper, write a brief intention for protection, such as "I am surrounded by a shield of safety and strength."
3. **Invoke the Elements:** Stand before your altar, take a deep breath, and say:
   "Earth, Air, Fire, Water, I call upon you to create a circle of protection around me.
   With salt of the Earth, I anchor my shield;
   With feather of Air, I guard my mind;
   With flame of Fire, I burn away harm;
   With water of Life, I flow in safety.
   By the power of the elements, this space is protected."

4. **Seal the Circle:** Place the paper with your intention in the center of the altar and hold your hands over the elements. Visualize a glowing shield of energy forming around you and your space.
5. **Close the Ritual:** Leave the stones in place for 24 hours to solidify the protection, then keep them in a special place, such as a pouch or on your altar, to maintain the spell's energy.

Customizations: Replace the feather, candle, salt, or water with items that represent the elements to you. For example, use a shell for water or a leaf for earth. Add symbols or sigils to the paper to personalize the spell further.

2. Self-Love Ritual: Rose Quartz Mirror Meditation
Purpose: To enhance self-love, acceptance, and inner peace.
Ingredients:

- A rose quartz crystal
- A mirror (handheld or small table mirror)
- A pink candle
- Rose-scented oil or lotion

Instructions:

1. **Prepare the Space:** Cleanse your space using your preferred method (smudging, sound, etc.). Place the mirror and rose quartz on your altar or table.
2. **Anoint the Candle:** Rub a few drops of rose oil onto the pink candle while visualizing love and acceptance flowing into your life. Light the candle and place it beside the mirror.
3. **Hold the Crystal:** Sit comfortably and hold the rose quartz in your hand. Close your eyes and take a few deep breaths, focusing on the energy of love emanating from the stone.
4. **Mirror Affirmations:** Open your eyes and look into the mirror. Hold the rose quartz to your heart and say aloud:
   "I am worthy of love and respect.
   I embrace my beauty, inside and out.
   I honor my journey and trust in my strength."
5. **Meditate:** Gaze into your own eyes in the mirror for several moments. Visualize a soft pink light glowing from your heart, expanding outward to surround you in a warm, loving embrace.
6. **Close the Ritual:** Blow out the candle, thanking it for its light and energy. Keep the rose quartz in your pocket or under your pillow to carry the self-love energy with you.

Customizations: Use different colored candles for varying intentions (e.g., green for healing, white for purity). Substitute rose quartz with another crystal, such as amethyst for self-understanding or citrine for confidence.

3. Abundance Spell: Prosperity Jar

Purpose: To attract wealth, prosperity, and abundance into your life.

Ingredients:

- A small jar with a lid
- Coins (preferably gold or silver-colored)
- Bay leaves
- Cinnamon stick
- Green candle
- Honey or sugar
- A piece of paper and green pen

Instructions:

1. **Cleanse the Jar:** Cleanse the jar by passing it through incense smoke or placing it under running water for a few moments. This clears any lingering energy from previous uses.
2. **Add Ingredients:** Begin filling the jar with the prosperity ingredients:
    - Place the coins in the bottom as symbols of wealth.
    - Add a bay leaf for luck and a cinnamon stick for financial success.
    - Drizzle a bit of honey or sprinkle sugar into the jar to "sweeten" your prosperity.
3. **Write Your Intention:** On the piece of paper, write your intention for abundance using the green pen. Fold the paper and place it into the jar.
4. **Seal the Jar:** Close the jar tightly and hold it in your hands. Light the green candle and say:

"Abundance flows to me with ease,
By Earth, Air, Fire, and Seas.
This jar of wealth I now create,
Brings fortune's blessings at every gate."

5. **Charge the Jar:** Allow the candle to burn for a few minutes while visualizing your intention filling the jar with glowing, golden light. Extinguish the candle and place the jar in a prominent place in your home, such as near your front door or on your altar.

6. **Ongoing Activation:** Shake the jar gently whenever you want to activate its energy or when you need an extra boost of prosperity.

Customizations: Add other symbols of abundance, such as small gemstones (e.g., citrine, green aventurine) or essential oils (e.g., patchouli, basil) to the jar.

4. Dream Enhancement Ritual: Moonlit Dream Sachet
Purpose: To enhance vivid dreams and facilitate dream recall.
Ingredients:

- Small fabric pouch
- Dried herbs (mugwort, lavender, chamomile)
- Moonstone or amethyst crystal
- Blue or purple thread
- A small slip of paper and pen

Instructions:

1. **Prepare the Herbs:** Place the dried herbs into a small bowl, mixing them with your hands while focusing on your intention to enhance your dreams.
2. **Fill the Pouch:** Add the herbs and the moonstone or amethyst crystal into the fabric pouch.
3. **Write Your Intention:** On the slip of paper, write your intention, such as "I invite vivid, meaningful dreams and clear recall." Fold the paper and place it into the pouch.
4. **Sew the Pouch:** Use the blue or purple thread to sew the top of the pouch closed. As you stitch, chant:
   "By moon and star, dreams take flight,
   Bring forth visions deep and bright.
   I open my mind to see and hear,
   Wisdom through dreams, crystal clear."
5. **Charge the Sachet:** Place the sachet under the moonlight overnight to charge it with lunar energy.
6. **Use the Sachet:** Place the sachet under your pillow or beside your bed to encourage vivid dreams and enhance dream recall.

Customizations: Replace or add other herbs based on your needs, such as rosemary for protection in dreams or jasmine for prophetic visions.

5. Seasonal Ritual: Yule Candle Blessing

Purpose: To welcome the return of the sun and manifest hope, joy, and warmth during Yule.

Ingredients:

- A gold or red candle
- Cinnamon powder
- Clove oil
- Evergreen sprig (pine, fir, or holly)
- A small bowl

Instructions:

1. **Anoint the Candle:** Rub a few drops of clove oil onto the candle, visualizing warmth and joy spreading through your space.
2. **Prepare the Blessing Powder:** In the bowl, mix a small amount of cinnamon powder with an affirmation for abundance, such as "As the sun returns, so does my joy and prosperity."
3. **Bless the Candle:** Roll the candle in the cinnamon powder while saying:
   "Golden light of Yule's rebirth,
   Bring warmth and joy upon the Earth.
   As this candle's flame does glow,
   My hopes and dreams begin to grow."
4. **Light the Candle:** Place the candle on your altar and light it, allowing its warmth to fill the room. Visualize the returning sun bringing new opportunities, energy, and hope into your life.
5. **Close the Ritual:** Let the candle burn for at least a few minutes, then extinguish it. Keep the candle on your altar and light it daily until it has burned completely, focusing on your intentions each time.

Customizations: Change the herbs or oils to match the season or Sabbat. For example, use lavender and mint for Imbolc or rosemary and sage for Samhain.

These sample spells and rituals offer a variety of magical practices that you can tailor to your specific intentions and preferences. Use them as inspiration to create your own unique rituals, blending ingredients, chants, and correspondences that resonate with your energy. Remember that the most powerful magic is personal, so feel free to adapt these examples in ways that reflect your journey and craft.

Appendix B: Magical Symbols Reference Guide: A Glossary of Common Sigils, Runes, and Icons

Magical symbols have been used throughout history as powerful tools for focusing intent, invoking energies, and conveying mystical concepts. They can be drawn, carved, painted, or incorporated into spells and rituals to enhance their power. This reference guide provides an overview of common sigils, runes, and icons used in various magical practices. Understanding these symbols and their meanings can enrich your spellcraft, providing you with a diverse toolkit for infusing magic into your daily life.

1. Sigils

Sigils are personal symbols created to represent a specific intention or desire. They are often used in spells, talismans, and ritual work to focus and direct energy toward a goal. While each practitioner's sigils are unique, certain traditional sigils have been used for centuries.

1.1 The Witch's Knot

- **Meaning:** Protection, warding off negativity, binding unwanted influences.
- **Description:** The Witch's Knot is composed of intertwining loops, forming a continuous, endless pattern. It represents the interconnectedness of all things and is often used to protect the home or sacred space from harmful energies.
- **Use:** Draw the Witch's Knot on doorways, windows, or objects for protection. It can also be added to amulets or talismans to shield the wearer from negative influences.

1.2 The Pentacle

- **Meaning:** Balance, protection, unity of the elements (Earth, Air, Fire, Water, Spirit).
- **Description:** A five-pointed star enclosed within a circle. Each point of the star corresponds to one of the five elements, symbolizing harmony and balance within the universe.
- **Use:** The pentacle is widely used in ritual work, often drawn on the ground or on an altar to create a sacred space. Wearing a pentacle as jewelry or incorporating it into spellwork brings protection, grounding, and spiritual alignment.

1.3 The Sigil of the Archangel Michael

- **Meaning:** Protection, courage, overcoming obstacles.
- **Description:** An intricate symbol featuring crossed lines, circles, and angular shapes. This sigil is associated with Archangel Michael, known for his role as a protector and guardian.
- **Use:** Draw this sigil on candles, amulets, or within your spellbook to invoke courage and protection. It is especially useful in rituals for banishing negativity or shielding yourself from harm.

1.4 Personal Sigils

- **Meaning:** Custom intentions or desires, unique to the individual.
- **Description:** Personal sigils are created by reducing a phrase or intention (e.g., "I am protected") into a symbolic design. This often involves combining or abstracting letters, shapes, and lines to form a unique symbol.
- **Use:** Once crafted, personal sigils can be drawn on candles, written in your spellbook, or used in meditation. Activate them by

focusing on the symbol while setting your intention, and then release it into the universe.

2. Runes

Runes are ancient symbols from the Norse and Germanic traditions,
often used in divination, spellwork, and talisman-making. Each rune
carries its own unique energy and meaning, offering insight and guidance.

2.1 The Elder Futhark Runes

The Elder Futhark is the oldest known runic alphabet, consisting
of 24 symbols. Here are a few key runes and their meanings:

2.1.1 Fehu (◈)

- **Meaning:** Wealth, prosperity, abundance, new beginnings.
- **Description:** Shaped like an angular "F," Fehu is associated with
  material wealth, financial success, and the manifestation of goals.
- **Use:** Carve or draw Fehu on money-related items, prosperity jars,
  or talismans to attract abundance and financial growth.

2.1.2 Ansuz (◈)

- **Meaning:** Communication, wisdom, divine inspiration.
- **Description:** Resembles an angular "A" and is connected to the
  god Odin, symbolizing knowledge, eloquence, and the power of
  words.
- **Use:** Incorporate Ansuz into spells or rituals involving communication, learning, or seeking guidance from higher sources.

2.1.3 Algiz (◈)

- **Meaning:** Protection, defense, higher self.
- **Description:** Looks like an upward-pointing branch or antlers. It represents a protective shield, invoking spiritual guardianship and defense against harm.
- **Use:** Draw Algiz on doors, windows, or objects to create a protective barrier. It can also be carried as a talisman for personal protection.

2.1.4 Berkano (◈)

- **Meaning:** Growth, fertility, new beginnings, nurturing energy.
- **Description:** Shaped like a rounded "B," Berkano is associated with birch trees and represents growth, renewal, and feminine energies.
- **Use:** Use Berkano in rituals for fertility, healing, or to nurture new projects. It is especially effective in spells for personal growth and spiritual development.

2.1.5 Ehwaz (◈)

- **Meaning:** Movement, progress, partnership.
- **Description:** Looks like an angular "M," symbolizing the horse and rider partnership. It represents forward movement, trust, and cooperation.
- **Use:** Incorporate Ehwaz into spells for travel, advancing projects, or strengthening relationships. It is also helpful in meditations focusing on personal growth and transformation.

3. Common Magical Icons and Their Meanings

Magical icons are symbols drawn from various mystical traditions, each carrying specific energies and meanings. These symbols can be used in spellwork, rituals, and the decoration of your spellbook.

3.1 The Triple Moon

- **Meaning:** The Goddess, cycles, intuition, the phases of life (maiden, mother, crone).
- **Description:** A central full moon flanked by two crescent moons (one waxing, one waning). It represents the three aspects of the Goddess and the cyclical nature of life.
- **Use:** The Triple Moon is commonly used in Wiccan and pagan practices to honor the feminine divine. Draw this symbol in your spellbook or on your altar to connect with the moon's energy, enhance intuition, and embrace the cycles of change.

3.2 The Ankh

- **Meaning:** Life, immortality, spiritual enlightenment.
- **Description:** An ancient Egyptian symbol resembling a cross with a loop at the top. It represents the key of life and eternal existence.
- **Use:** Use the Ankh in rituals related to healing, vitality, and spiritual growth. It can also be worn as an amulet to promote balance and harmony in life.

3.3 The Triskelion (Triple Spiral)

- **Meaning:** Motion, personal growth, life cycles, the interconnectedness of mind, body, and spirit.
- **Description:** Three interlocking spirals radiating from a central point. The triskelion symbolizes the triad nature of existence: past, present, future; life, death, rebirth.
- **Use:** Draw the triskelion in spells or meditations focusing on progress, transformation, and the journey of self-discovery. It is also used to invoke the energies of the Triple Goddess.

3.4 The Eye of Horus

- **Meaning:** Protection, healing, wisdom, insight.
- **Description:** An ancient Egyptian symbol resembling a stylized eye. It represents the eye of the god Horus, symbolizing protection, health, and restoration.
- **Use:** Incorporate the Eye of Horus into protection spells, health rituals, or as a personal sigil for insight and spiritual vision. It can be drawn on amulets or worn as jewelry to safeguard against negativity.

3.5 The Spiral

- **Meaning:** Growth, evolution, the journey of life, cosmic energy.
- **Description:** A continuous, coiling line that radiates outward from a central point. The spiral represents the natural patterns of growth, the cycle of life, and the path of spiritual development.
- **Use:** Draw the spiral in rituals for personal transformation, spiritual awakening, or to manifest continuous progress in a particular

area of life. It can also be used in meditative practices to connect with the flow of cosmic energy.

4. Alchemical Symbols

Alchemical symbols represent elements and substances in traditional alchemical practices. They are often used in spells, rituals, and talisman-making to align with the energies of these elements.

4.1 The Alchemical Elements

- **Earth (◈):** Symbolized by an inverted triangle with a line through the top. Represents stability, grounding, fertility, and material aspects of life.
  - ○ **Use:** Incorporate this symbol in grounding rituals, prosperity spells, or talismans for protection.
- **Water (◈):** Depicted as an inverted triangle. Symbolizes emotions, intuition, purification, and the subconscious.
  - ○ **Use:** Use in spells for emotional healing, divination, or cleansing rituals.
- **Air (◈):** Shown as an upright triangle with a line through the middle. Represents intellect, communication, and the breath of life.
  - ○ **Use:** Integrate this symbol into rituals for mental clarity, communication enhancement, or inspiration.
- **Fire (◈):** Represented by an upright triangle. Associated with passion, transformation, courage, and creative energy.
  - ○ **Use:** Include in spells for strength, purification, or to ignite passion and drive in life.

Using Symbols in Your Practice

These symbols serve as powerful tools for focusing intent and manifesting your desires. You can use them in a variety of ways:

- **In Spellcraft:** Draw or carve symbols into candles, stones, or parchment to empower spells and rituals.
- **On Tools:** Inscribe symbols onto your magical tools, such as wands, athames, or chalices, to enhance their energy.
- **In Your Spellbook:** Add these symbols to the pages of your spellbook as decorative elements, protective seals, or reminders of their meanings. You can also create a "symbol of the week" section to explore a new symbol's energy and incorporate it into your practice.

Understanding the meanings and uses of these common sigils, runes, and icons empowers you to deepen your magical work and personalize your spells. This glossary serves as a starting point, providing you with a foundational toolkit to explore, adapt, and expand upon in your own magical journey.

Appendix C: Supplies and Resource List: Where to Find Materials for Crafting

Crafting a spellbook is a creative and magical process that requires a variety of supplies, from inks and papers to herbs, crystals, and other enchanting materials. Sourcing high-quality items can greatly enhance the energy and aesthetics of your spellbook. This appendix provides a detailed list of supplies needed for crafting your spellbook and offers guidance on where to find them. Whether you're looking for specialty shops, online stores, or natural sources, this resource list will help you gather everything you need.

1. Writing Supplies and Paper

1.1 Blank Notebooks, Journals, and Scrapbooks

- **What to Look For:** Choose high-quality paper that can withstand different types of ink, paint, and adhesives. Look for acid-free or archival-quality paper to ensure the longevity of your spellbook.
- **Where to Find:**
  - **Local Art Supply Stores:** Many art supply stores carry a wide selection of journals and sketchbooks with varying paper textures and weights. Brands like Moleskine, Strathmore, and Canson offer durable options.
  - **Bookstores:** Some bookstores carry unique journals, including leather-bound books and handmade paper notebooks. Check specialty sections or shops that focus on metaphysical, spiritual, or artistic themes.
  - **Online Stores:** Websites such as **Etsy, Amazon**, and **Paperblanks** offer a range of journals, from ornate leather-bound books to minimalist designs.
  - **Specialty Craft Stores:** Stores like **Michaels** and **Hobby Lobby** often stock blank scrapbooks and journals in their crafting and papermaking sections.

1.2 Handmade and Aged Paper

- **What to Look For:** Handmade paper has a unique texture that adds an antique, mystical quality to your spellbook. Look for papers made from natural fibers like cotton, hemp, or mulberry.
- **Where to Find:**
  - **Art Supply Shops:** Stores such as **Dick Blick Art Materials** and **Jerry's Artarama** carry handmade papers, including options with pressed flowers, fibers, or natural dyes.
  - **Etsy:** A treasure trove for handmade and specialty papers. Search for sellers who create handmade, aged, or tea-stained paper specifically for journaling or spellbook crafting.
  - **Papermaking Kits:** If you prefer to make your own paper, look for papermaking kits at art stores or online marketplaces. Making your own paper allows you to customize the color, texture, and inclusions (like herbs or flower petals).

1.3 Inks and Writing Tools

- **What to Look For:** Water-resistant inks are ideal for spellbook entries that need to last. Consider colored inks for different magical correspondences (e.g., green for abundance, red for passion).
- **Where to Find:**
  - **Art Supply Stores: Dick Blick**, **Michaels**, and **Joann Fabrics** offer a wide selection of inks, including India ink, calligraphy ink, and pigment-based markers.
  - **Stationery Shops:** Many specialty stationery shops carry fountain pen inks, dip pens, and calligraphy sets.

- ○ **Online Retailers: Goulet Pens, JetPens**, and **Amazon** provide a variety of ink colors, calligraphy tools, and fountain pens.
- ○ **Etsy:** For enchanted or handmade inks, search on Etsy for sellers who craft magical inks infused with herbs, oils, or moon water.

2. Embellishments and Decorative Supplies
2.1 Ribbons, Tassels, and Bookmarks

- **What to Look For:** Silk, satin, or velvet ribbons in colors that correspond with your intentions. Consider adding tassels, charms, or beads for a personalized touch.
- **Where to Find:**
    - ○ **Craft Stores: Michaels, Hobby Lobby**, and **Joann Fabrics** offer an extensive selection of ribbons, tassels, and beads in various colors, materials, and widths.
    - ○ **Fabric Shops:** Stores like **Fabric.com** or local fabric shops often carry specialty ribbons and trimmings that can be used to create bookmarks or embellishments.
    - ○ **Etsy:** Find handcrafted tassels, ribbon bookmarks, and charms made by artisans who focus on magical or bohemian crafting themes.

2.2 Wax Seals and Stamps

- **What to Look For:** Wax seal kits with a variety of seal designs (e.g., pentacles, moons, initials) and wax sticks in different colors (e.g., gold, silver, red).
- **Where to Find:**
    - ○ **Stationery Stores:** Specialty stores like **Paper Source** and **Kate's Paperie** often carry wax seal kits, stamps, and a variety of colored wax sticks.

- **Online Marketplaces:** Websites like **Etsy, Amazon**, and **Nostalgic Impressions** provide wax seal kits, including traditional symbols and custom designs.
- **Craft Stores:** Larger craft stores like **Michaels** and **Joann Fabrics** often stock sealing wax and stamp sets in their paper crafting sections.

2.3 Gold Leaf, Foil, and Embossing Supplies

- **What to Look For:** Gold leaf sheets, metallic foils, embossing powders, and adhesive size for gilding edges, creating sigils, or adding decorative touches.
- **Where to Find:**
  - **Art Supply Stores: Dick Blick** and **Jerry's Artarama** carry gold leaf, adhesive size, embossing powders, and heat guns.
  - **Craft Stores: Michaels** and **Hobby Lobby** offer gold leaf sheets, foil, embossing kits, and heat tools in their papercraft or painting sections.
  - **Etsy:** For unique foil patterns and embossed designs, search on Etsy for handmade foil sheets and embossing tools crafted by artists.

2.4 Dried Flowers, Herbs, and Pressed Elements

- **What to Look For:** Dried flowers, herbs, and foliage for decorative embellishments. Choose botanicals that correspond with the spells or energies you wish to work with (e.g., lavender for peace, rosemary for protection).
- **Where to Find:**
    - **Herb Shops:** Local apothecaries, herbal stores, or farmers' markets often sell dried herbs in small quantities.
    - **Etsy:** Search for dried flowers, herbs, and pressed plants. Many sellers specialize in ethically sourced or organically grown botanicals.
    - **Craft Stores: Michaels** and **Joann Fabrics** sometimes carry dried flowers and foliage in their floral or wedding sections.
    - **DIY:** Gather and press your own flowers and herbs by placing them between parchment paper inside heavy books. This adds a personal touch and infuses your spellbook with your energy.

3. Crafting Tools
3.1 Paper Trimmers, Scissors, and Craft Knives

- **What to Look For:** High-quality cutting tools for shaping pages, trimming edges, or creating pop-ups and compartments within your spellbook.
- **Where to Find:**
  - **Craft Stores: Michaels, Joann Fabrics**, and **Hobby Lobby** offer a variety of scissors, craft knives, and paper trimmers.
  - **Art Supply Stores: Dick Blick** and **Jerry's Artarama** carry professional-grade cutting tools.
  - **Online Retailers: Amazon** and **CraftDirect** provide a wide selection of cutting tools, including specialty scissors with patterned edges.

3.2 Adhesives and Binding Supplies

- **What to Look For:** Acid-free, archival-quality adhesives that won't damage your spellbook over time. Look for glue sticks, double-sided tape, binding glue, or fabric glue for different crafting needs.
- **Where to Find:**
  - **Craft Stores: Michaels, Joann Fabrics**, and **Hobby Lobby** have extensive adhesive options, including glue sticks, double-sided tape, binding glues, and specialty glues.
  - **Bookbinding Suppliers: Hollanders** and **Talas** are specialty bookbinding stores that offer high-quality adhesives, tools, and materials for binding and repairing books.

3.3 Stencils, Stamps, and Stickers

- **What to Look For:** Stencils for drawing sigils, stamps for adding symbols, and stickers for decoration.
- **Where to Find:**
    - ◦ **Craft Stores: Michaels, Joann Fabrics**, and **Hobby Lobby** carry stencils, stamps, ink pads, and a variety of stickers.
    - ◦ **Etsy:** Search for handmade stencils and stamps, especially those with magical or mystical designs. Many artisans create custom or themed stamps that add a unique touch to your spellbook.
    - ◦ **Online Marketplaces: Amazon, AliExpress**, and **Scrapbook.com** offer an array of stickers and stamps suited for spellbook crafting.

4. Natural Materials and Tools for Spellcraft
4.1 Herbs, Crystals, and Essential Oils

- **What to Look For:** Herbs and oils that correspond with your magical practices, such as lavender for relaxation or rose quartz for love spells. Choose ethically sourced crystals and high-quality essential oils.
- **Where to Find:**
    - ◦ **Herbal Shops and Apothecaries:** Local herbal stores or metaphysical shops often carry a variety of dried herbs, essential oils, and crystals.
    - ◦ **Online Stores: Mountain Rose Herbs, The Crystal Council**, and **Bulk Apothecary** offer a vast selection of herbs, oils, and crystals, often with detailed information on sourcing and uses.

- **Etsy:** Many sellers on Etsy offer small batches of organically grown herbs, handmade essential oils, and ethically sourced crystals.
    - **Farmers' Markets:** Local markets can be a great source of fresh herbs, flowers, and natural materials for your spellbook.

4.2 Feathers, Bones, and Natural Finds

- **What to Look For:** Feathers, bones, shells, and other natural items that hold symbolic significance in your practice. Choose items collected ethically and respectfully from nature.
- **Where to Find:**
    - **Nature Walks:** Collect feathers, shells, stones, or wood pieces while respecting local wildlife and ecosystems. Clean and purify any items you bring home.
    - **Etsy:** Search for ethically sourced feathers, bones, and shells from sellers who follow ethical collection practices.
    - **Metaphysical Shops:** Some metaphysical stores carry ethically sourced natural items, including feathers, shells, and stones.

5. Specialty and Online Stores for Magical Supplies

Here are some recommended specialty and online stores where you can find a variety of magical crafting supplies:

- **The Magickal Cat:** Offers a range of metaphysical supplies, including crystals, herbs, ritual tools, and spellbook crafting materials.
- **Llewellyn Worldwide:** A renowned publisher of metaphysical and spiritual books, they also offer journals, candles, herbs, and ritual tools.

- **The Witches Moon:** A subscription box service that includes candles, herbs, oils, and tools for spellcrafting. Great for sourcing unique items for your spellbook.
- **Enchanted Earth:** An online store that provides a variety of magical items, including spell candles, incense, oils, herbs, and crystals.
- **Alchemy Works:** Specializes in traditional magical herbs, oils, seeds, and resins for spellcrafting and magical crafting.

By exploring these resources, you can find both common and unique materials to create and enhance your spellbook. Whether you seek basic supplies like ink and paper or specialty items like gold leaf and pressed herbs, this list provides a comprehensive guide to sourcing high-quality materials that will enrich your spellbook and magical practice. Remember, part of the magic is in the gathering and preparation of your tools, so enjoy the process as you build your collection!

Appendix D: Further Reading: Suggested Books and Online Resources for Spellbook Crafting and Witchcraft

Crafting a spellbook is a deeply personal and enriching experience, yet it's also rooted in centuries of magical tradition. To enhance your knowledge and skills, it's beneficial to explore a variety of resources on witchcraft, spellbook crafting, herbal magic, divination, and other esoteric subjects. This appendix provides an extensive list of recommended books and online resources for beginners and seasoned practitioners alike, offering diverse perspectives on the art of witchcraft and spellbook creation.

1. Books on Spellbook Crafting and Magical Writing

1.1 "The Grimoire Journal: A Place to Record Spells, Rituals, Recipes, and More" by Paige Vanderbeck

- **Overview:** This journal offers a structured yet flexible format for recording spells, rituals, and magical recipes. It's designed to inspire practitioners in documenting their magical practice, making it an excellent resource for those looking to craft their own spellbook.
- **Why It's Useful:** Provides practical prompts and templates for recording spells, meditations, and correspondences, helping you organize your spellbook effectively.
- **Where to Find:** Available on **Amazon, Barnes & Noble**, and other major book retailers.

1.2 "The Witch's Book of Self-Care: Magical Ways to Pamper, Soothe, and Care for Your Body and Spirit" by Arin Murphy-Hiscock

- **Overview:** This book offers spells, rituals, and practices for self-care, focusing on nurturing your physical, mental, and spiritual well-being. It includes recipes, meditations, and rituals that can be recorded in your spellbook.
- **Why It's Useful:** Encourages creating a section in your spellbook dedicated to self-care spells and rituals, providing inspiration for personalizing your magical journal.
- **Where to Find:** Available at major book retailers and online at **Amazon** and **IndieBound**.

1.3 "The Green Witch: Your Complete Guide to the Natural Magic of Herbs, Flowers, Essential Oils, and More" by Arin Murphy-Hiscock

- **Overview:** A comprehensive guide to green witchcraft that explores the use of herbs, flowers, essential oils, and stones in magical practice. The book provides spells, rituals, and correspondences that you can incorporate into your spellbook.
- **Why It's Useful:** Ideal for creating sections in your spellbook on herbal correspondences, botanical magic, and natural crafting.
- **Where to Find:** Available on **Amazon, Barnes & Noble**, and in many local bookstores.

1.4 "Grimoire for the Green Witch: A Complete Book of Shadows" by Ann Moura

- **Overview:** A detailed Book of Shadows that covers various aspects of witchcraft, including spells, rituals, herbal lore, divination, and the Sabbats. The book provides structured content for creating your own grimoire or spellbook.
- **Why It's Useful:** Serves as both a reference guide and a template for those creating a comprehensive, traditional-style spellbook.
- **Where to Find:** Available through **Amazon, IndieBound,** and **Books-A-Million.**

1.5 "The Element Encyclopedia of 5,000 Spells: The Ultimate Reference Book for the Magical Arts" by Judika Illes

- **Overview:** This extensive compendium contains thousands of spells, charms, incantations, and enchantments from various cultures and traditions.
- **Why It's Useful:** Provides a rich source of inspiration for crafting your own spells, rituals, and magical correspondences to include in your spellbook.
- **Where to Find:** Available at major booksellers like **Amazon, Barnes & Noble,** and **Book Depository.**

1.6 "The Witch's Journal: Charms, Spells, Potions and Enchantments" by Selene Silverwind

- **Overview:** A beautifully illustrated book filled with spells, charms, potions, and rituals. It includes sections on magical tools, herbs, stones, and seasonal celebrations.
- **Why It's Useful:** Offers creative ideas for enhancing your spellbook with visual elements like sigils, diagrams, and decorative borders.

- **Where to Find:** Available online at **Amazon** and in select local bookstores.

1.7 "A Witch's Guide to Crafting Your Practice: Create a Magical Path That Works for You" by Lisa McSherry

- **Overview:** This guide helps you tailor your magical practice to your personal preferences and lifestyle. It covers building a spiritual routine, creating a sacred space, and crafting spells that align with your unique path.
- **Why It's Useful:** Encourages a personalized approach to spellbook crafting, offering suggestions for creating rituals and spells that resonate with your own magical style.
- **Where to Find:** Available through **Amazon, IndieBound,** and **Barnes & Noble.**

2. Books on Witchcraft, Divination, and Magical Correspondences

2.1 "Encyclopedia of Magical Herbs" by Scott Cunningham

- **Overview:** This classic reference guide provides detailed information on over 400 herbs, including their magical properties, planetary correspondences, and uses in spells and rituals.
- **Why It's Useful:** Perfect for creating an herbal correspondence section in your spellbook. Provides detailed descriptions and correspondences that can be directly transcribed or adapted into your own entries.
- **Where to Find:** Available at **Amazon, IndieBound,** and in many metaphysical bookstores.

2.2 "Cunningham's Encyclopedia of Crystal, Gem & Metal Magic" by Scott Cunningham

- **Overview:** An in-depth look at the magical properties of crystals, gemstones, and metals. It includes correspondences and instructions on how to use these materials in various magical workings.
- **Why It's Useful:** Useful for crafting a section in your spellbook dedicated to crystal magic, with entries on the meanings, uses, and properties of different stones.
- **Where to Find:** Available through major book retailers like **Amazon, Barnes & Noble,** and **Book Depository.**

2.3 "The Modern Guide to Witchcraft: Your Complete Guide to Witches, Covens, & Spells" by Skye Alexander

- **Overview:** A contemporary introduction to witchcraft that covers spellcasting, the elements, moon phases, and ritual crafting. The book provides straightforward instructions for creating a magical practice.
- **Why It's Useful:** Helps beginners create sections in their spellbook on the basics of witchcraft, such as lunar phases, elemental magic, and foundational spells.
- **Where to Find:** Available on **Amazon, Books-A-Million,** and **IndieBound.**

2.4 "The Crystal Bible" by Judy Hall

- **Overview:** A comprehensive guide to the properties and uses of hundreds of crystals, including their healing and metaphysical properties.
- **Why It's Useful:** An invaluable reference for creating detailed entries on crystal correspondences in your spellbook, particularly for spells involving healing, protection, or meditation.

- **Where to Find:** Available at most bookstores, including **Amazon** and **Barnes & Noble**.

2.5 "Llewellyn's Complete Book of Correspondences: A Comprehensive & Cross-Referenced Resource for Pagans & Wiccans" by Sandra Kynes

- **Overview:** An extensive reference covering correspondences for the elements, planets, zodiac signs, deities, colors, crystals, herbs, and more.
- **Why It's Useful:** Provides a broad array of correspondences that can be incorporated into your spellbook's sections on spells, rituals, and magical theory.
- **Where to Find:** Available on **Amazon, Llewellyn Worldwide**, and other major book retailers.

3. Online Resources for Spellbook Crafting and Witchcraft
3.1 Learn Religions (https://www.learnreligions.com)

- **Overview:** Offers articles on various aspects of witchcraft, Wicca, and paganism, including spellwork, rituals, Sabbats, and magical correspondences.
- **Why It's Useful:** A free resource for learning about different traditions, practices, and spells, which can be adapted and recorded in your spellbook.

3.2 Witchipedia (https://www.witchipedia.com)

- **Overview:** An online encyclopedia of witchcraft terms, spells, herbs, crystals, and symbols. It covers a wide range of topics from spellcraft to divination techniques.
- **Why It's Useful:** Provides concise and accessible information on magical correspondences, symbols, and practices, which can be referenced in your spellbook.

3.3 The Green Witch's Cottage (https://thegreenwitchscottage.com)

- **Overview:** A blog and resource site focused on green witchcraft, herbal magic, and natural healing practices. Offers tips on using herbs, crystals, and moon phases in spellcraft.
- **Why It's Useful:** Ideal for creating entries in your spellbook related to herbal correspondences, natural magic, and seasonal spells.

3.4 Llewellyn Worldwide (https://www.llewellyn.com)

- **Overview:** A publisher of metaphysical books, Llewellyn's website features articles, resources, and information on witchcraft, tarot, astrology, and other esoteric topics.
- **Why It's Useful:** Offers book recommendations, guides, and free articles to enhance your knowledge of magical practices, providing inspiration for spellbook content.

3.5 YouTube Channels (e.g., The Witch of Wonderlust, HearthWitch, Scarlet Ravenswood)

- **Overview:** Many YouTubers specialize in witchcraft, offering tutorials on spellwork, spellbook crafting, herbal magic, and more.
- **Why It's Useful:** Visual guides for crafting your spellbook, demonstrating techniques like candle carving, sigil creation, and herbal preparation. Watching these tutorials can provide practical inspiration and ideas for personalizing your spellbook.

4. Online Stores for Witchcraft Supplies

While crafting your spellbook, you may want to source specialized supplies from reputable online stores:

- **The Magickal Cat** (https://www.themagickalcat.com): Offers a wide variety of witchcraft supplies, including candles, herbs, crystals, and ritual tools.
- **Llewellyn Worldwide** (https://www.llewellyn.com): In addition to books, Llewellyn sells tarot cards, journals, calendars, and other magical tools.
- **MysticConvergence.com** (https://www.mysticconvergence.com): Features a range of magical supplies, from spell kits to oils and altar tools.
- **Witchcrafts Artisan Alchemy** (https://www.witchcraftsartisanalchemy.com): Specializes in handcrafted candles, oils, and herbal blends for ritual use.

This reading list and collection of resources will help you deepen your understanding of witchcraft, enhance your spellcrafting skills, and inspire new entries for your spellbook. Whether you're exploring traditional practices or modern interpretations of magic, these books and online resources provide a wealth of knowledge to support your journey.

Conclusion

A spellbook is more than just a collection of spells and correspondences; it is a reflection of your personal journey as a practitioner of magic. Creating a handmade spellbook is an act of devotion, creativity, and self-expression. By infusing your intentions, energy, and knowledge into its pages, your spellbook becomes a living testament to your magical practice. As you continue to explore the realms of witchcraft, this sacred book will evolve alongside you, serving as a guide, a companion, and a repository of your magical experiences.

The Power of a Handmade Spellbook: Reflecting Your Personal Journey

Throughout this guide, you've learned how to craft a spellbook that resonates with your unique energy and practice. Every element—from the cover design to the symbols and spells within—serves as a mirror of your personal journey. As you write, draw, and embellish its pages, you are not only documenting your path but also creating a magical tool that holds the power of your intentions, dreams, and spiritual growth.

A handmade spellbook captures the essence of your magical work and experiences. It becomes a sacred space where you can freely explore your thoughts, emotions, and spiritual insights. The process of crafting it teaches patience, focus, and the art of imbuing objects with intention. It encourages you to engage deeply with your practice, turning each page into a physical representation of your spiritual energy. The more effort, care, and intention you pour into your spellbook, the more powerful and meaningful it becomes.

Your spellbook is also a testament to your progress. As you flip through its pages in the future, you'll be reminded of the spells you've cast, the rituals you've performed, and the lessons you've learned. Each entry will be a marker of your evolution, illustrating how your knowledge, skills, and connection with the craft have grown over time. This living document will continue to transform as you add new spells, record your experiences, and deepen your magical understanding.

Encouraging Creativity and Individuality in Crafting

There is no one right way to craft a spellbook. The beauty of this practice lies in its infinite possibilities for creativity and self-expression. From choosing the perfect book base and designing the cover to adding mystical symbols, illustrations, and personal notes, every step of the process is an opportunity to infuse your individuality into your spellbook. It is an extension of who you are as a witch, healer, or spiritual seeker.

Your spellbook doesn't have to conform to any particular tradition or style. It can be a minimalist notebook with simple ink drawings or a lavishly adorned tome with intricate embossing, pressed herbs, and gilded edges. The key is to create something that resonates with you and supports your magical practice. Incorporate elements that speak to your soul—whether it's using colors that correspond with your intentions, including favorite crystals, or adding affirmations and poetry that uplift your spirit.

This guide has provided you with techniques and inspiration for crafting a spellbook, but remember that the most powerful magic comes from within. Let your intuition guide you as you fill its pages. Experiment with different methods, materials, and designs. Use your spellbook to explore new aspects of magic, document your experiences, and refine your craft. As you grow more confident, you'll find that the process of creating and using your spellbook becomes a deeply personal and transformative ritual in itself.

Next Steps: Exploring Witchcraft Practices and Rituals with Your New Spellbook

Now that you have your handcrafted spellbook, the next phase of your journey begins. With your spellbook in hand, you are equipped to delve deeper into the mysteries of witchcraft and explore a wide range of practices, from herbal magic and moon rituals to divination and energy work. This magical tool will serve as both a guide and a record, helping you navigate new territories with intention and focus.

Here are some steps you can take to further your exploration:

- **Start a Daily or Weekly Practice:** Use your spellbook to track your magical practices, such as daily affirmations, moon phase observations, tarot readings, and meditation exercises. Regular entries will help you connect with the rhythms of nature and deepen your intuition.
- **Document Your Spellcasting:** When casting spells, take the time to write down the ingredients, steps, and intentions in your spellbook. Afterward, document the results and any observations you make. This practice will help you refine your spellcasting techniques and understand what works best for you.
- **Expand Your Knowledge:** Use the "Further Reading" appendix in your spellbook as a resource for deepening your understanding of magical practices. As you learn about new symbols, correspondences, or rituals, incorporate them into your spellbook to create a rich and comprehensive resource tailored to your path.
- **Create Seasonal and Sabbat Entries:** As the Wheel of the Year turns, use your spellbook to explore and celebrate each Sabbat. Write down rituals, spells, and reflections that align with the energies of the seasons. This practice will help you attune to the natural cycles and incorporate seasonal magic into your life.
- **Develop Personal Rituals:** Use your spellbook to experiment with creating personal rituals that resonate with your goals and

spiritual needs. Whether it's a daily grounding meditation, a monthly cleansing ritual, or a full moon spell, recording these practices will help you establish a meaningful routine.

- **Revisit and Reflect:** Periodically revisit the pages of your spellbook to reflect on your journey. Review past spells and rituals, noting what worked, what didn't, and what insights you've gained. Use this reflection to adapt and evolve your magical practices.

Your spellbook is now ready to be filled with your magic, creativity, and exploration. As you continue on your path, remember that this book is a sacred space—a place where your thoughts, dreams, spells, and knowledge come together to form a tapestry of your spiritual journey. Allow it to be a canvas for your evolving craft, a source of inspiration, and a magical companion that grows and transforms with you.

Blessings on your journey, and may your spellbook become a beacon of wisdom, power, and enchantment that guides you in all your magical endeavors.

Message from the Author:

I hope you enjoyed this book, I love astrology and knew there was not a book such as this out on the shelf. I love metaphysical items as well. Please check out my other books:

-Life of Government Benefits

-My life of Hell

-My life with Hydrocephalus

-Red Sky

-World Domination:Woman's rule

-World Domination:Woman's Rule 2: The War

-Life and Banishment of Apophis: book 1

-The Kidney Friendly Diet

-The Ultimate Hemp Cookbook

-Creating a Dispensary(legally)

-Cleanliness throughout life: the importance of showering from childhood to adulthood.

-Strong Roots: The Risks of Overcoddling children

-Hemp Horoscopes: Cosmic Insights and Earthly Healing

- Celestial Hemp Navigating the Zodiac: Through the Green Cosmos

-Astrological Hemp: Aligning The Stars with Earth's Ancient Herb

-The Astrological Guide to Hemp: Stars, Signs, and Sacred Leaves

-Green Growth: Innovative Marketing Strategies for your Hemp Products and Dispensary

-Cosmic Cannabis

-Astrological Munchies

-Henry The Hemp

-Zodiacal Roots: The Astrological Soul Of Hemp

- Green Constellations: Intersection of Hemp and Zodiac

-Hemp in The Houses: An astrological Adventure Through The Cannabis Galaxy

-Galactic Ganja Guide

Heavenly Hemp

Zodiac Leaves

Doctor Who Astrology

Cannastrology

Stellar Satvias and Cosmic Indicas

Celestial Cannabis: A Zodiac Journey

AstroHerbology: The Sky and The Soil: Volume 1

AstroHerbology:Celestial Cannabis:Volume 2

Cosmic Cannabis Cultivation

The Starry Guide to Herbal Harmony: Volume 1

The Starry Guide to Herbal Harmony: Cannabis Universe: Volume 2

Yugioh Astrology: Astrological Guide to Deck, Duels and more

Nightmare Mansion: Echoes of The Abyss

Nightmare Mansion 2: Legacy of Shadows

Nightmare Mansion 3: Shadows of the Forgotten

Nightmare Mansion 4: Echoes of the Damned

The Life and Banishment of Apophis: Book 2

Nightmare Mansion: Halls of Despair

Healing with Herb: Cannabis and Hydrocephalus

Planetary Pot: Aligning with Astrological Herbs: Volume 1

Fast Track to Freedom: 30 Days to Financial Independence Using AI, Assets, and Agile Hustles

Cosmic Hemp Pathways

How to Become Financially Free in 30 Days: 10,000 Paths to Prosperity

Zodiacal Herbage: Astrological Insights: Volume 1

Nightmare Mansion: Whispers in the Walls

The Daleks Invade Atlantis
Henry the hemp and Hydrocephalus

10X The Kidney Friendly Diet
Cannabis Universe: Adult coloring book
Hemp Astrology: The Healing Power of the Stars
Zodiacal Herbage: Astrological Insights: Cannabis Universe: Volume 2
Planetary Pot: Aligning with Astrological Herbs: Cannabis Universes: Volume 2
Doctor Who Meets the Replicators and SG-1: The Ultimate Battle for Survival
Nightmare Mansion: Curse of the Blood Moon
The Celestial Stoner: A Guide to the Zodiac
Cosmic Pleasures: Sex Toy Astrology for Every Sign
Hydrocephalus Astrology: Navigating the Stars and Healing Waters
Lapis and the Mischievous Chocolate Bar

Celestial Positions: Sexual Astrology for Every Sign
Apophis's Shadow Work Journal: : A Journey of Self-Discovery and Healing
Kinky Cosmos: Sexual Kink Astrology for Every Sign
Digital Cosmos: The Astrological Digimon Compendium
Stellar Seeds: The Cosmic Guide to Growing with Astrology
Apophis's Daily Gratitude Journal

Cat Astrology: Feline Mysteries of the Cosmos
The Cosmic Kama Sutra: An Astrological Guide to Sexual Positions
Unleash Your Potential: A Guided Journal Powered by AI Insights
Whispers of the Enchanted Grove

Cosmic Pleasures: An Astrological Guide to Sexual Kinks

369, 12 Manifestation Journal

Whisper of the nocturne journal(blank journal for writing or drawing)

The Boogey Book

Locked In Reflection: A Chastity Journey Through Locktober

Generating Wealth Quickly:

How to Generate $100,000 in 24 Hours

Star Magic: Harness the Power of the Universe

The Flatulence Chronicles: A Fart Journal for Self-Discovery

The Doctor and The Death Moth

Seize the Day: A Personal Seizure Tracking Journal

The Ultimate Boogeyman Safari: A Journey into the Boogie World and Beyond

Whispers of Samhain: 1,000 Spells of Love, Luck, and Lunar Magic: Samhain Spell Book

If you want solar for your home go here: https://www.harborso-lar.live/apophisenterprises/

Get Some Tarot cards: https://www.makeplayingcards.com/sell/ apophis-occult-shop

Get   some   shirts: https://www.bonfire.com/store/apophis-shirt-emporium/

Instagrams:
@apophis_enterprises,
@apophisbookemporium,
@apophisscardshop
Twitter: @apophisenterpr1
Tiktok:@apophisenterprise
Youtube: @sg1fan23477, @FiresideRetreatKingdom

Podcast: Apophis Chat Zone: https://open.spotify.com/show/5zXbrCLEV2xzCp8ybrfHsk?si=fb4d4fdbdce44dec

Newsletter: https://apophiss-newsletter-27c897.beehiiv.com/

9 798330 463824